Bloom's
GUIDES

Arthur Miller's
Death of a Salesman

1984
All the Pretty Horses
Beloved
Brave New World
Cry, the Beloved Country
Death of a Salesman
Hamlet
The Handmaid's Tale
The House on Mango Street
I Know Why the Caged Bird Sings
The Scarlet Letter
To Kill a Mockingbird

Bloom's
GUIDES

Arthur Miller's
Death of a Salesman

Edited & with an Introduction
by Harold Bloom

CHELSEA HOUSE
P U B L I S H E R S
A Haights Cross Communications Company

Philadelphia

© 2004 by Chelsea House Publishers, a subsidiary of Haights Cross Communications.

A Haights Cross Communications Company

Introduction © 2004 by Harold Bloom.

Printed and bound in the United States of America.

First Printing
1 3 5 7 9 8 6 4 2

Library of Congress Cataloguing-in-Publication Data applied for.

ISBN: 0-7910-7564-8

Chelsea House Publishers
1974 Sproul Road, Suite 400
Broomall, PA 19008-0914

www.chelseahouse.com

Contributing editor: Portia Williams Weiskel
Cover design by Takeshi Takahashi
Layout by EJB Publishing Services

Contents

Introduction

HAROLD BLOOM

The dramatic critic Eric Bentley defines the central flaw in *Death of a Salesman* as Arthur Miller's inability (and consequently ours) to know whether the play's obsessive concern is politics or sex. Bentley's point is accurate, and the assertions of some feminist critics that Willy Loman's tragedy centers on "the politics of sex" seem to me unpersuasive. As a playwright, Arthur Miller works always in the shadow of Henrik Ibsen, a dangerous influence for Miller because Ibsen essentially was a daemonic dramatist, trollish and Shakespearean, always closer to a cosmos of elemental forces, like those in *King Lear* and *Macbeth*, than to the social world of politics and economics. Even Ibsen's social dramas conceal trollish energies behind their societal masks; Hedda Gabler is more a troll than a victim of the patriarchy, and can be regarded as Iago's sister. But Miller always has imitated what he interprets as a social reformer in Ibsen, forgetting James Joyce's wry observation that Ibsen was no more a feminist than Joyce was a bishop. Social forces certainly affect Hedda Gabler, but Ibsen does not represent them as controlling her life or as determining her fate. Miller, in contrast, wants to give us a Willy Loman who is destroyed by social energies. Fortunately for the continued dramatic validity of *Death of a Salesman*, something deeper than Miller's political polemic pervades the play and makes it more than a parody of "the American Dream" of upward mobility, so that Willy Loman finally escapes the dubious fate of being a poor man's Jay Gatsby.

For a dramatic protagonist to impress us as legitimately "tragic," she or he must possess aesthetic dignity, which is not necessarily identical with human dignity. All bad tragedies, as Oscar Wilde might have said, are sincere, and Arthur Miller's sincerity is palpable. Miller has written some bad tragedies, but *Death of a Salesman* certainly is not one of them. With all its faults and ambiguities, it rivals Eugene O'Neill's *Long Day's*

Journey into Night as a modern American tragic drama, even though, like O'Neill's work, it seems to me of a lesser eminence than the best tragicomedies of Tennessee Williams. Like O'Neill, Miller essentially is the tragedian of what Sigmund Freud called "Family Romances." *Death of a Salesman* is more the tragedy of a family than it is of an individual or of a society. Doubtless I am influenced by the experience of once having attended a performance of the play in Yiddish translation, which I found to be both illuminating and harrowing, though highly ironic, since Miller labors in his drama to render Willy as the American Everyman and the Lomans as an archetypal American family. Perhaps Miller succeeds in this effort, though at a certain cost, by blending Willy and the Lomans into a common grayness, so that they lack all color or exuberance and yield much of their pathos to a vision of social reductiveness, as if they were victims purely of the false dreams of their nation. What *Death of a Salesman* most lacks is a Shakespearean or Ibsenite *foregrounding*: a sense of the involvement of tradition both in Willy's loneliness and in his family's inability to understand his yearning quality, his dream of an excessive familial love that might assuage his loneliness.

Even though Willy Loman's aesthetic dignity depends more upon pathos than upon a nonexistent tragic grandeur, his dignity seems to me real enough to have sustained the play and to go on sustaining it for some years to come. Miller's social ironies mostly weaken the drama, yet the ironies of familial love in *Death of a Salesman* constitute its ongoing strength. Though it is forty-four years since I saw the play in its Yiddish version, I remain seared by the peculiar power of that performance, which accentuated the anguish of the Lomans' family romance and the dignity of Willy's desperate failure to be what he yearned to be, a good father and a good husband. If Willy has tragic stature, it is because he is exiled from himself, and so can win no victory whatsoever. We are terribly moved by Willy's confused conviction that, if he is not successful, then he will not deserve to be loved by his family. No possible success could assuage Willy's tormented yearning to be popular, to be loved. It is a peculiar tragedy that Willy is destroyed by love, and by the inevitable ambivalences that attend family romances. The American dream in Jay Gatsby is a High Romantic vision of Eros, grotesquely represented by his nostalgia for the banal Daisy, and yet still an authentic vision, because Gatsby himself, as mediated by the narrator Nick Carraway, is anything but banal. Willy Loman's American dream is rescued from aesthetic banality precisely because it is possessed by the enigmas that mark a guilty dream. Poor Willy, who desired so intensely only to be a good husband and a good father, destroys himself because of the guilty realization that pragmatically he has become both a bad husband and a bad father. I do not think that Willy Loman has the authentic dignity of a tragic protagonist, but his sincere pathos does have authentic aesthetic dignity, because he does not die the death of a salesman. He dies the death of a father, perhaps not the universal father, but a father central enough to touch the anguish of the universal. ∎

Biographical Sketch

Born in Manhattan on October 17, 1915, Arthur Miller was the second of three children for Isadore and Augusta Miller, a well-to-do Jewish couple. In 1929 the stock market crash and Depression forced his father out of the coat business and their family out of their home to a small frame house in Brooklyn. Upon graduating from Abraham Lincoln High School in 1932, Miller started saving as much as he could from his income at an auto-parts warehouse so he could go to college. He occasionally would read on the subway on his way to work, and when he happened upon Dostoevsky's *The Brothers Karamazov*, Miller "all at once believed [he] was born to be a writer."

But when he applied to the University of Michigan, Miller was turned down until he tried for a third time with a convincing letter he sent to the admissions officer. Having heard the school gave writing prizes, he enrolled in journalism, and within eighteen months he began writing plays, winning the Avery Hopwood Award on his first try for a piece he had written in just four days, *Honors at Dawn*. He received another Hopwood for his second work, *No Villain*, just one year later in 1937.

After he received his B.A. in 1938, Miller went back to New York and worked with the Federal Theatre Project until it was abolished; he then ended up on welfare. He completed his play, *The Golden Years*, and to make money he wrote numerous radio scripts—work he hated. In 1940 Miller married Mary Grace Slattery, to whom he had become engaged at the University of Michigan; they moved to Brooklyn and eventually had two children. He held various odd jobs and kept writing for the next four years, while she served as the main breadwinner, working as a waitress and editor.

In 1944, his first Broadway production took place. The play's title, *The Man Who Had All the Luck*, certainly wasn't applicable to Miller at the time, for the piece struggled through only six performances, although it managed to win the Theatre Guild National Award. A back injury kept Miller out of the military, but he visited army camps during the war and published his journal, *Situation Normal*, in 1944. By 1945 Miller switched gears and wrote a novel, *Focus*, about anti-Semitism. He became increasingly involved in leftist organizations and liberal causes. Then in 1947 his first son was born, and his first successful Broadway play was produced, *All My Sons*. It showed the after-effects of World War II on a family whose father had sold faulty plane parts to the government.

But Miller's most famous play by far became *Death of a Salesman*, which centered on a dejected salesman's final days. It was composed in six weeks on a typewriter Miller had bought with the money he earned from his first Hopwood. That year—1949—the Pulitzer Prize was awarded for the first time—to Miller. He also received the New York Drama Critics' Circle Award for the work, which continued through 1950 for 742 performances. The same year Miller traveled to California to work on a film project. He met Marilyn Monroe and they saw each other frequently for many weeks.

In 1951 Miller published an adaptation of Henrik Ibsen's *An Enemy of the People*. Political commitments took up much of Miller's time then, and in 1953 he put his warnings about the dangers of mass hysteria and government power into the form of *The Crucible*, a work about the Salem witch trials that was readily construed as a metaphor for the McCarthy hearings then taking place. By 1955 Miller's marriage was falling apart, and he met Monroe again at a theater party. They were seen together more often, and he was divorced that year. Miller married Marilyn Monroe in 1956.

The Crucible was well-received, but it helped bring Miller negative attention of another sort. In June of 1956 he was subpoenaed to come before the House Un-American Activities Committee. Curiously, in the midst of his political troubles, he announced that he and Monroe had been secretly married. Before the Committee, Miller freely admitted his past associations with leftist groups, stating they had ended in 1950. He went further and refused to be a "good citizen" who would identify other Communists. He named not one.

During this time, in 1955, Miller saw his *A View from the Bridge* produced on a double bill with a short play, *A Memory of Two Mondays*. He also won his second Pulitzer Prize. His screenplay for the 1961 film *The Misfits* was created for his wife, who starred in it with Clark Gable, but shortly thereafter in that same year, they were divorced. Also in that year, Miller's mother died at the age of eighty.

In 1962, Miller married the photographer Inge Morath, with whom he had two children and collaborated on several books, writing text to accompany her images. By 1964, Miller's *After the Fall* was produced, creating more controversy than any of his previous work. Many critics balked at what they construed to be an excessively autobiographical piece.

Miller covered the Nazi trials in Frankfurt for the *New York Herald Tribune* and then wrote *Incident at Vichy* (1965), a short play about Nazism and anti-Semitism in Vichy France. In the same year he traveled extensively in Europe to oversee productions of his various works.

In 1966 approximately seventeen million viewers saw *Death of a Saleman* on television, twenty times the number who had seen the play when it was on Broadway. A collection of short stories, *I Don't Need You Anymore* (1967) followed, and another play, *The Price* (1968). He was a member of the Connecticut delegation to the fateful Democratic National Convention in 1972, and he continued to be politically active and speak out for his beliefs. In 1973 the comic *The Creation of the World and Other Business* was produced, as well as the *The Archbishop's Ceiling* (1977) and *The American Clock* (1980).

In 1983 Miller directed *Death of a Salesman* in China. *Up from Paradise* was published in 1984, followed by *Danger: Memory!* in 1986, and his autobiography, *Timebends: A Life*, in 1987. He continued to see his works published and produced not only in theater but also on television. In 1994 *Broken Glass* was published, and in 1995 production began on a film version of *The Crucible*.

Miller continues to write in his Connecticut home. Dustin Hoffman, one of the most famous Willy Lomans, describes Miller in *Arthur Miller and Company* as "so articulate. He's this great storyteller. He sounds like this New York cab driver; he's so unpretentious and earthy. You're laughing one minute, then you're thinking the next, and touched the next."

The Story Behind the Story

During a rehearsal of *Death of a Salesman* in Beijing using Chinese actors for a Chinese audience, Arthur Miller suddenly stood up, stopped the play, and made a speech to all assembled about his feelings for the character of Willy Loman. Miller was pleased by the progress of actor Ying Ruocheng's portrayal of Willy as "... a little bantam with quick fists and the irreducible demand that life give him its meaning and significance and honor." (*"Salesman" in Beijing* 49) But he was disappointed that the entire company had not yet succeeded in animating the poetic vision of the play. He quotes himself:

> ... [T]he one red line connecting everyone in the play was a love for Willy; not admiration necessarily, but a kind of visceral recognition that in his fumbling and often ridiculous way he is trying to lift up a belief in immense redeeming possibilities. (49)

Acknowledging that Willy was often irascible and not always deserving of emulation, Miller articulated what has become the most common response to his most famous character: "[Willy] is the walking believer, the bearer of a flame whose going-out would leave us flat." (49)

By the time Miller arrived in China to direct his play (1983), *Salesman* had been playing continuously to appreciative audiences since its opening on February 10, 1949, at the Morosco Theatre in New York City. The play instantly generated controversy, focusing mainly on two questions: Can the classical definitions of tragedy—involving persons of great stature and elevated consciousness brought down by a combination of fate and personal flaw—be properly expanded and updated to include the suffering and downfall of Willy Loman, indisputably a common man? And, can the play be understood as an indictment of American capitalism? Although Miller has commented extensively on these issues, his interest in the play has tended more to the question of its universality.

Recent feminist criticism has questioned whether the perceived marginalization of women in the play—especially Linda—both dates and diminishes the work, but Miller was attempting to accurately reflect the times, and in any case his question still stands: Is Willy's story emblematic of a human aspiration recognizable to people of all nations? This was the challenge that brought him to Beijing.

Salesman had played successfully to many foreign audiences, but the desecration of art carried out in the Cultural Revolution by Mao's wife Jiang Qing and the Gang of Four had left an entire generation of Chinese bereft of any awareness of world literature or culture. Theatre people like Ruocheng were banished to rice farms leaving the people with Jiang Qing's simplistic "Eight Permissible Plays." If one in four human beings is Chinese, Miller reminds us, hope for "universality" must confront alien concepts and daunting difficulties with translations. Miller struggled with transmitting culture-bound concepts like the link between suicide and insurance money for Biff and had to accept Willy's impassioned, "I won't take the rap for this" to be translated, "I won't carry this blackened cooking pot on my back." In the end, however, despite a few alarmed moments of anticipating that "the whole effort would end in calamity" (viii), Miller and his Chinese colleagues produced *Salesman* to an appreciative Chinese audience. Full of emotion, the audience responded with prolonged applause and did not seem to care that the last buses home were leaving without them. Miller was exhilarated to have this confirmation of his belief in one humanity.

Interestingly, in no other play except Wilder's *Our Town* do American dreams, contradictions, and history figure so centrally. June Schleuter's essay in *Approaches to Teaching Miller's "Death of a Salesman"* provides a useful chronology. Willy was born in 1886, and his brother Ben was born in 1873. In 1880, their father deserted the family, heading to Alaska, not to be seen again. The Loman family drama is rooted in the myth and reality of the American West when it was still possible to wander without destination, seeking to subdue the land and claim its riches for one's own.

Willy grounded his life in a different success myth, historically associated with Horatio Alger's rags-to-riches novels that would have been selling by the millions during Willy's formative years. Building on Ben Franklin's cheery certainty that hard work, discipline, and character would lead to personal success ("The Way to Wealth" speech in *Poor Richard*, 1758) and Emerson's essay "Self-Reliance" (1841), Alger, a clergyman, expanded the myth to include the dubious but liberating notion that achieving material success was God's intention for humankind. American identity—both spiritual and public—was engaged by this mythology. "Success is a requirement Americans make of life," wrote critic Henry Popkin, mentioning Willy. (Henry Popkin, *Sewanee Review* LXVII. Winter, 1960, p. 53)

The American Dream functions almost like a character in *Salesman*, but in the words of critic Thomas E. Porter:

> Miller uses this [American Dream] model in order to subvert it. His play is an anti-myth, the rags-to-riches formula in reverse so that it becomes the story of a failure in terms of success, or better, the story of the failure of the success myth. (Porter 131)

This darker side of American life received less publicity than the success myth but was the inevitable consequence of postwar capitalist competition in an expanding economy. For some to win in this system others had to lose. And for readers interested in overlapping explanations for Willy's failures, images from the Depression are instructive. Miller recalled for a BBC interview in 1995 three Depression-era suicides on his Brooklyn block. "These people," he said, "were profound believers in the American Dream. The day the money stopped their identity was gone." (Qf. *The Cambridge Companion to Arthur Miller* 1)

Two Americans—one in anticipation, the other in retrospection—seemed to have had in mind a person like Willy Loman when writing about the American experience. Thoreau's early lines in *Walden* (1854)—"The mass of men lead lives of quiet desperation"—evoke an image of Willy as we might imagine him spending a lifetime of bone-wearying hours in his car or hotel room, planning his next move, figuring his day's commission. And Willy with his social awkwardness, self-doubt, and abruptly changing emotional states fits David Riesman's description in *The Lonely Crowd* (1969) of the "inner-directed" person trying to fit into an "other-directed" society. Riesman described the subsequent loss of personhood and mental disintegration as "anomie." Both observations shed light on Willy's poignant and memorable self-description to his older brother Ben: "... I still feel kind of temporary about myself."

Salesman came into being almost overnight. In the summer of 1948 Miller was working fitfully on another play when suddenly, from several unrelated parts of his life, a stream of images and ideas coalesced into a play about a salesman. The original title—*The Inside of His Head*—reflected Miller's intention to present a drama of personal downfall from a purely subjective viewpoint, but it was abandoned after he found himself engaged in more complex themes.

The compelling script attracted the attention of Elia Kazan, the famous director who had just concluded a successful run of Tennessee Williams' *A Streetcar Named Desire*. Several commentators have enjoyed reporting on the elaborate efforts made by Mildred Dunnock, a slight and elegant actress, to win the part of Linda, pictured by Miller as dowdy, like one who lived in her housedress. Lee J. Cobb was the first "Willy." To impart the dignity and gravity deemed appropriate to the "Willy" character, Miller and Kazan took Cobb to a performance of Beethoven's *Seventh Symphony* the afternoon of *Salesman*'s first performance. Despite warnings from some promoters that the title was too morose to attract—and might even repel—audiences, the play ran for 742 performances. It won that year's Pulitzer Prize and numerous other awards, and put Arthur Miller firmly on the American scene.

List of Characters

Arthur Miller tells us that **Willy Loman** has a mercurial nature and turbulent dreams. Son Happy tells us that Willy is happiest when looking forward to something. Linda likens him to "only a little boat looking for a harbor." To her, he is "the dearest man in the world ... [and] the handsomest." To son Biff, Willy is both a "prince" and a "phony little fake." Willy indignantly insists that he is "not a dime a dozen"; but he also feels "kind of temporary about [himself]." The question of the play is: Who is Willy and why does his life turn out as it does? Fatherless father of Biff and Happy, husband of Linda, Willy is the (not especially talented) traveling salesman responsible for the New England territories. His characteristic bravado masks a disabling insecurity which drives him to make fanciful claims; e.g. the Providence police personally protect his parked car, and to live vicariously though his sons, especially Biff, his favorite. Now in his sixties, stoop-shouldered and exhausted, Willy is hours away from being fired when we meet him and a few more hours away from planting seeds where no sun will shine and then taking his own life. The name "Willy Loman" has become almost synonymous with the American Dream— both the high hopes and the hopes dashed and all the energy associated with its attainment.

Biff Loman, the older of Willy's sons, moves from being the popular and promising high school football hero to a 34-year-old small-time thief and occasional farmhand. At the time of the play Biff is—and has been—struggling to put his life in order. Ambivalent about his father and therefore about himself, "lost" Biff faces the pressure of choosing a life and career that will satisfy his own nature or one that will win his father's approval. Some critics regard Biff's role in the play as equivalent to Willy's because Biff must consciously act on the issues and dilemmas that destroy his less self-aware father. Certainly their destinies are intertwined. Emotionally paralyzed and fated to carry the family secret, Biff has nonetheless achieved sufficient self-knowledge to be able to dismiss Happy's description of him as "idealistic" in favor of the more truthful "mixed up very bad." The play does not condemn Biff for his impulse to whistle in elevators or go off swimming in the middle of the day. Ben Franklin would have worried about Biff but Walt Whitman would have enjoyed his companionship.

Happy Loman, the younger son, not only does not whistle in elevators, he castigates brother Biff for doing so because—he insists—such acts of spontaneous whimsy do not get one hired in the business world. In the shadow of Biff's high school glory, Happy is frequently seen—through Willy's recollected episodes—struggling for his father's attentions. As an adult, Happy has fallen unimaginatively (though with different illusions) into a self-gratifying version of Willy's career path. Both sons are tall, fit, and attractive to women, but Miller gives to Happy the role of exuding the sexuality that is otherwise a hidden and problematic theme in the play. Happy idealizes his mother and treats other women with callous bravado and self-indulgence. His concern for Willy prompts him to pay for a respite trip to Florida, but his refusal to publicly recognize his distraught father in the restaurant is an act of astonishing cruelty.

Linda Loman, wife and mother in the family, appears to take a passive role in the play, but she has generated her own share of controversial commentary, especially by critics. Some see her as admirable and selfless for taking the role encouraged for postwar women of returning to domestic life to provide stability and emotional support for the American family. Others see her as pathetic and marginalized (along with the other women in the play) by the male characters. Difficulty in understanding Linda is exacerbated by her reticence about herself. Aware in a way that the others are not of the precariousness of the family, she has understandably placed Willy's problems at the center of her life. Miller tells us she has an "iron repression" but does this indicate long-suffering love or resentment, exhaustion, a fierce will, or defeat? In Beijing Miller insisted that Linda be played as the kind of woman "... who is strong by concealing her strength." (*"Salesman" in Beijing* 87) Indisputable and unwavering is Linda's love for Willy, but some aspects of her behavior seem irrational and self-defeating: why, for example, would one encourage a beloved spouse to continue in his exaggerations and self-deceptions? Despite her "I don't understand" speech at the gravesite, Linda possesses more of the facts of the play than the other characters and her "Attention must be paid" speech is among the most famous in American drama.

In Willy's delusional episodes his older brother Ben (**Uncle Ben**) appears as a living character. We learn later that Ben has died, apparently fairly recently. His ghostly appearances during Willy's final days of life provide important insights about Willy's character and why he has become who he is. Director Elia Kazan persuaded Miller to change Ben's role to de-emphasize his influence on Willy as the stand-in father for their deserted family in order to amplify his sensational qualities as the embodiment of the American success myth. Ben is fabulously rich and more damaging than useful as a father replacement. Ben's signature lines—"... [W]hen I was seventeen I walked into the jungle, and when I was twenty-one I walked out. And by God I was rich."—convey his rapacious opportunism. And his advice to Biff—"Never fight fair with a stranger, boy. You'll never get out of the jungle that way."—conveys his compromised ethics. Although we only know about Ben what Willy's selective memory presents, he appears to have misused the concept of "self-reliance" to justify his belligerent self-aggrandizement. Although married with children, Ben acts like one without emotional ties; he barely tolerates Willy, is plainly disdainful of Linda, and interacts with his nephews only by showing off his questionable ethics. Without Ben in the play we would never know about Willy's origins which are clearly implicated in the tormenting conflicts and confusion he has endured most of his life.

As Willy's longtime neighbor and friend, **Charley** is the unlikely poetic defender of the salesman's dreams and easy to characterize as the "decent capitalist" in the play. He appears to have played fair and been moderately successful. Charley has, however, and by his own admission, paid a price for his success: "My salvation is that I never took any interest in anything." Since Willy began faltering on the job Charley has quietly been "loaning" him money to pay the bills and even offers him a job. He enjoys teasing Willy but always affectionately; no matter how exasperating Willy is, Charley remains a friendly and concerned neighbor. Charley's presence at the funeral as the only non-relative in attendance harshly contrasts with the image carried by Willy all these years of the adoring admirers of legendary salesman Dave Singleman gathered for his funeral.

Son of Charley and friend, neighbor, and classmate of the Loman boys, **Bernard** provides a telling contrast to Biff. Never athletic in high school, "liked" but not "*well* liked," studious and conscientious, instead—these features, scorned by Willy and his boys at the time, turn out to have served Bernard well. While grown-up Biff is floundering, Bernard is a practicing lawyer with a case currently before the Supreme Court. Bernard also functions in the play as witness to Biff's *un*promising characteristics in high school and to the traumatic effect on Biff of his fateful visit to Willy in Boston in the summer of 1932. Remarkably, although Bernard was frequently in the shadow of the Loman brothers, he has always exhibited more concern for them than resentment. He does, however, know that "You can't get something for nothing," as Biff does not.

Howard, son of Willy's original boss, has the brief but pivotal role of firing Willy just at the moment Willy is hopefully asking for the less strenuous job of non-traveling salesman. In this capacity Howard is often castigated as the callous capitalist but he is also—and perhaps more disturbingly—an ordinary man, like Willy, a proud father of two. Willy has, in fact, not been performing well for the business, but it is difficult not to regard as an inexcusable cruelty Howard's oblivious disregard of Willy's desperate plight. Howard is mesmerized by his new gadget, the tape-recorder, and so focused on protecting his "bottom line" that he doesn't appear even to see Willy. Willy with his second-to-last hope is eclipsed in this scene, reduced to nothing.

Summary and Analysis

Contribution of Stage Design to Theme

Only moments into the play we know the essential story: a salesman—not ill but clearly exhausted and discouraged, and introduced incongruously by pleasantly pastoral music—will die by the end of the play. Before the audience hears a word of dialogue, the stage design has provided this framework for Willy's life with the use of one auditory and one visual device. The auditory clue—the "... melody ... played upon a flute.... telling of grass and trees and the horizon"—contrasts harshly with the visual clue—the image of Willy's modest house menacingly dwarfed (again, the incongruity) by the "towering, angular" apartment buildings that now surround it. Someone accustomed to horizons and wide open spaces is likely inclined to think adventurously, even to dream of wild possibility. But one whose window "opens" onto a building which forms part of a "solid vault" of similar view-obstructing buildings is likely to feel like a caged spirit, like one not quite alive. Willy—we come to learn—is both of these people.

Director Elia Kazan said of Willy: "[He is] one vast contradiction ... and this contradiction is his downfall." He and set designer Jo Mielziner joined their talents with Miller's to create a powerful and evocative setting that would reflect Willy's contradictory nature and dilemma. Miller's original stage image of a large head opening to reveal a "mass of contradictions" would have been an effective Expressionistic device for dramatizing a single disintegrating mind, but Miller's view of life and art precluded reducing a person to a disintegrating mind or human existence to a jumble of subjective experiences. The set as it finally evolved blended features of Realism and Expressionism with a result so rich in symbolism and significance, both emotional and historical, that critic Enoch Brater wrote, "In a very real sense, the set is Miller's play." (Brater 119) The stage design made possible the subjective enactment of Willy's suffering in a context that invited audiences to reflect on what objective historical and

23

economic circumstances may have contributed to the downfall of this quite ordinary American citizen.

Willy's house, for example, is not even his own, nor is his death. Both belong explicitly to a "Salesman." Such a deliberate reference recalls the observation commonly made by native and foreign America-watchers alike that Americans think of themselves in terms of what they do; their identity is their job title. According to this view, the "real self" or "inner nature" is undervalued, even betrayed, in service to the profit-making economic system. English critic Raymond Williams articulates one version of this political view of *Salesman*:

> ... in the end it is not Willy Loman as a man, but the image of the Salesman.... that sums up the theme referred to as alienation, for this is a man who from selling things has passed to selling himself, and has become, in effect ... a commodity which like other commodities will at a certain point be economically discarded.
> (Corrigan, ed. 75)

From a related perspective, Miller scholar Linda Kintz points out the implied message of rejection located in the sight of Willy's little plot of earth and isolated domicile left behind by America's prideful urbanization. She writes:

> Built into that message is the inherent contradiction between an admonition to be number one, which Willy takes seriously, and the inevitability that there will be far more losers than winners, a message he hears only too late. (Bigsby, ed. 104)

In the Introduction to his *Collected Plays*, Miller acknowledges that he intentionally left unclear what Willy was carrying in his salesman's bags ("Himself") but insists that no explicit political view or overt program for social reform motivated his writing the play. The set design is equally suited to dramatizing public and private issues and particularly the synergy created when they overlap. The varying musical themes closely follow Willy's inner state of mind. The "angry orange" and lonely blue colors on stage and the sheltering leafy overlay highlighting family life in Brooklyn before it became a claustrophobic "asphalt jungle" are subjective and objective indicators of Loman family life. The spatial juxtaposition of rooms on stage permits intimate and simultaneous views of Linda alone in her bedroom worrying about Willy—who is audibly mumbling to himself in the kitchen—while the grown sons briefly back together in their old bedroom engage in a disjointed conversation consisting of crude "guy talk" and alarm about their father. The kitchen table signifies American family life. The refrigerator that breaks down first because it is new and getting itself "worked in" and then because it is old evokes the era of time payments and frustration with cheap and falsely advertised gadgets. Biff's athletic trophy is now tellingly located not in the boys' room but in Willy's. The otherwise uncluttered stage leaves the most space for the dramatization of Willy's escalating madness.

Function of Time Sequences

Death of a Salesman consists of three parts, two acts and the Requiem, and encompasses three time sequences. The play opens and closes in historical time—the year 1949. Both acts blend this linear time scheme with fragments of past time which Willy not so much recalls as re-enters to re-live for purposes that serve both himself and the audience. The audience comes to understand that Willy's departures from linear time are a response to a deep need within himself for self-understanding. These episodes also make possible Miller's critical interest in providing the view from inside Willy's head. The characters' sometimes realistic, sometimes phantasmal actions around doors and walls are visible markers for the shifting time dimensions in Willy's mind. A third category of time is a non-sequential dimension. Episodes occurring in this category consist of merged fragments of past and present time that engulf Willy with increasing frequency and intensity as the boundaries in his mind dissolve. These skillfully constructed scenes provide external manifestations of Willy's mental disintegration and some clues about why it is occurring.

The Requiem, by contrast, provides the distance—locatable in objective time and space—from which Willy's survivors and the audience may ponder and comment upon the meaning of his death.

Willy's Crisis

Act One opens as Willy, dressed in his salesman's clothes, is returning home after another in a series of recently-occurring failed business trips. His exhaustion and sense of defeat blend with Linda's barely suppressed alarm. Willy's return marks the beginning of the last day of his life. At the time, however, despite the air of urgency surrounding him, only Linda has reasons for premonition and her days have been consumed with frantic strategies to save her husband's life.

Willy is a man carrying the weight of many losses. Miller describes him as coming home to "let his burden down" but coming home also brings him face to face with the most tormenting of his losses: his relationship with son Biff. Willy has lost his grip on life; he has literally lost his grip on his car which seems to him to be steering itself off the road. Willy has just spent most of his day inside of it, lost and dangerously disoriented. The car—central symbol of success in American culture and literally of vital importance for a salesman—is no longer under Willy's control.

Willy's implausible excuse for his abnormal behavior—an odd cup of coffee—reveals how far he has strayed from his own senses. As we watch Linda's response to Willy in this first scene, we see she has joined him in his disordered thinking as well—maybe it's his glasses or the steering mechanism of the car—but she has done so to keep the appearance of normality when she knows otherwise. One may come to question the wisdom or appropriateness of Linda's interventions with Willy (or the absence of them), but she is clearly animated by a fierce and loyal love for her husband. Suggesting to Willy that taking an aspirin will help him feel better exposes her desperate state of mind. Linda is at the outer limit of her capacity to cope with Willy's condition. Other sources of help—professional or familial—that might have been available are, for reasons of history or personal fate, not available to her.

Also in this first scene, Willy exposes some elements of the pattern his desperation has taken: explosive bouts of self-contradiction (Biff is lazy, Biff is not lazy) and vacillation between defeat ("I just couldn't make it....") and little spasms of feigned hope ("I'm vital in New England"). Within the latter comment one also hears the measure of Willy's self-deception. Using the only resources they can summon, Willy and Linda create a kind of false consciousness about the turmoil at the center of their lives.

Willy is unmistakably afflicted with many of the now classic signs of depression. He has lost his capacity for concentration and remembering; he cannot drive and confuses his current car with the one belonging to the family in 1928. But these are symptomatic losses pointing to far more disruptive losses in Willy's life. He speaks "with wonder" of the scenery and sunshine he encounters more abundantly the farther north—away from his home and the city—he travels. The simple pleasures of beauty and warmth put Willy into a reverie so deeply satisfying that he falls into a private mental region where there are no longer any cars or roads. The power of this reverie to put Willy's life in danger suggests that some vital inner deprivation has overtaken his conscious life. Indeed, evoked first by the flute music, a profound lament runs through the entire play for the loss of open space, a wide sky, and real earth under ones feet.

Once back in his house Willy demands to have opened the already open windows; nothing can alleviate his sense of being "boxed in" with "windows and bricks." We readily infer that the Lomans were unable to afford the land next door and therefore impotent to save from destruction two well-loved elm trees by an impersonal, almost mechanical "they." Willy's "sense of place"—a defining ingredient of the American dream experience observed by prominent scholars of American culture from deToqueville to Wendell Berry—has been violated. The degree of bitterness generated by this kind of loss is heard in Willy's choice of words: "They massacred the neighborhood."

"They" *have* massacred this neighborhood and thousands like it. But who is this "they"? Willy is right to connect this heart-wrenching loss to runaway population growth but he has neither the intellect nor the self-awareness to recognize the contradiction inherent in his angry sadness; namely, that the material wealth promised by the American Dream which Willy equates with "success" is delivered through the system of capitalism, which requires ever increasing growth in population and consumption, which in turn ensures the paving over of America, building lot by building lot, and the irrevocable loss of a profound source of personal happiness. No character in the play reflects directly on this paradox of American life—although each one is affected by it. Audiences and critics, however, do reflect on these and related issues raised by the play, and these observations are part of the once-heated and still ongoing commentary about the play. Miller, like the Greeks, wanted his plays to have a social impact without being polemical. In *Death of a Salesman* it's not a contest of ideas we are observing but rather the complexities of people's lives as they consciously and unconsciously embrace and resist the prevailing influences of the time.

Willy's keenest and most disabling loss is his relationship with son Biff. At the time of the play, 34-year-old Biff has returned home in nearly as much turmoil about starting a life as Willy is of concluding his. A shift of light focuses on Biff and Happy in their bedroom, both now out of bed, unable to sleep after overhearing the agitated talk coming from below. Their conversation exposes a genuine sibling bond despite the marked differences in their personalities. Also exposed are the remarkable similarities between Biff and his father. Like Willy, Biff is both driven and paralyzed, dominated by feelings of shame, guilt, anger, and determination. Both express an unsatisfied desire for connection to the land and open spaces. Biff can find satisfying work on a Texas ranch but finds himself each spring suddenly ensnared in self-doubt "about not gettin' anywhere!" Happy, by contrast, claims to enjoy the outdoor life but his enthusiasm is compromised by male narcissism and an unapologetic preference for making money. Above all Happy is eager for conquest and self-aggrandizement and appears indifferent about using callous and indecent means to make his impression. He imagines, for example, humiliating his merchandise manager by out-boxing him in the middle of the store and boasts to Biff about seducing the soon-to-be bride of an executive of the business. Unlike Biff, Happy is self-deceived—naming his aggression "an overdeveloped sense of competition"—and quick to idealize—calling "poetic" Biff's anguished speech about the newborn Texas colts which Biff insists on calling being "mixed up very bad." Both brothers are (with different emphasis) skeptical about equating happiness with wealth; they share (with equal emphasis) an expanding anxiety about Willy. Hints about a dark secret carried by Biff are introduced and hastily dropped in this scene.

What emerges in these early episodes is an unarticulated conflict between two American ideals: the pursuit of happiness through connection to the land (associated with homesteading and frontier life) and the pursuit of happiness associated with the acquisition of material wealth. As the play unfolds we notice that the ethical systems governing each ideal are inherently incompatible. The ensuing conflict is re-enacted especially acutely in Biff and Willy but generally in the whole family and by implication the whole nation.

Arthur Miller scholar, M. C. Roudané points out the numerous instances in the play "in which Willy's body language and dialogue create images of the fall, the falling, or the fallen." (Bigsby, ed. 66) Our first impression of Willy is of a man on the verge of collapse. He "sinks" into a chair, appears "beaten down," and, in Act Two, is abandoned on the floor of a restaurant, "on his knees." As we absorb the accumulating weight of these images we may also become aware of an invisible kind of falling: Willy's recurring lapses into other dimensions of time.

Miller's Use of Time in Act One

American thinking has traditionally emphasized linear progress in the form of a belief in starting over and getting a second chance. Early manifestation of this thinking is found in the fervor the new settlers felt for overthrowing the old ways of England and Europe, and in the notions of "rags-to-riches" and "Manifest Destiny." Some American writers have worked against this grain. One thinks of William Faulkner's famous line—"The past is not dead; it's not even past."—that occurs in a speech by the perspicacious narrator Gavin Stevens in *The Town* (1957) and F. Scott Fitzgerald's insight about the futility of trying to escape the past conveyed through the famous concluding images of *The Great Gatsby* (1925). Arthur Miller stands in this tradition of American writers. He studied the Greek playwrights and Henrik Ibsen during his college years and was impressed by their similar obsession with the "presentness" of the past. The objective events of *Salesman* are enacted over a period of 24 hours but the play derives its intensity from the novel intermingling of past and present sequences of experience that create a sense of Willy Loman beyond chronological time. We are privileged in this manner to get as close as possible to the eternal nature of another human being.

In his Introduction to *The Collected Plays* Miller writes, "*Death of a Salesman*" [is founded upon] the concept that nothing in life comes 'next' ... everything exists together and at the same time within us; ... there is no past to be 'brought forward' in a human being ... he is in his past at every moment...." (*Collected Plays* 23) An innovative artist, Miller saw the potential in blending the different representations of time used in Expressionistic and Realistic theatre, that is to say, mingling sequences of subjective and chronological time, for dramatizing a more complete and genuine measure of human feeling. In *Arthur Miller And Company* Miller states, "I've come out of the playwriting tradition which is Greek and Ibsen where the past is the burden of man and it's got to be placed on the stage so he can grapple with it." (*Arthur Miller and Company* 201) Earlier he stated, "[The] job of the artist is to remind people of what they have chosen to forget." (200)

When asked about his artistic methods of presenting time, Miller has frequently cited the pivotal moment in his career when he met by chance his Uncle Manny as both were emerging from a showing in Boston of *All My Sons*. Without even a greeting, Manny began to cry and then speak about his own son without any explicit reference to whatever in the play had churned up his thoughts. Miller called it "non-transitional speech" and immediately saw its poetic possibility for the theatre. The episode had for Miller the quality of epiphany and its impact explains the title he gave his 1987 autobiography— *Timebends*—where he writes:

> How fantastic a play would be that did not still the mind's simultaneity, did not allow a man to 'forget' and turned him to see present through past and past through present, a form that in itself, quite apart from its content and meaning, would be inescapable as a psychological process and as a collecting point for all that his life in society had poured into him. (*Timebends* 131)

Because time has a central importance for Miller in general and for this play in particular, more discussion differentiating the issue is helpful. "Flashback" is the customary term for the technique of including scenes from the past to illustrate meaning in the present. But this is not what is happening to Willy. The action in the two acts moves in concert with Willy's wandering thoughts. On this point Elia Kazan wrote, "There are no flashbacks....The only laws of these scenes are the laws of Willy's mind. And all the figures in Willy's mind are distorted by Willy's *hopes, wishes, desires*." (Rowe 44)

The presence of the past in the present disorders chronological time but does not make it less legitimate. Miller's integration of these memory sequences into the dialogue ("non-transitional speech") allows the audience to observe— and almost to experience—the way in which elements from Willy's past, both happy and ominous, combine with his increasingly frantic hopes for the future. The consequence for Willy is disorientation to the point of impotence. And it is exactly what we see: Willy unable to make anything happen— on the road; with his sons; with Linda who disobeys his sharp command to throw out the torn stockings; and, in Act Two, with his boss; and out in his almost sunless little patch of backyard, trying to make seeds grow. The intensity of Willy's vacillation between euphoria and dismay deprives him of rational thought and self-control and makes of his present life a sustained torture of self-doubt and recrimination. Miller has effectively produced in this play a heightened sense of reality, of the full reality of Willy's state of mind in these moments: the dramatization of insanity. Miller has this to say about Willy in his lapses:

> [Willy] was the kind of man you see muttering to himself on a subway, decently dressed, on his way home or to the office, perfectly integrated with his surroundings excepting that unlike other people he can no longer restrain the power of his experience from disrupting the superficial sociality of his behavior. Consequently he is working on two logics which often collide. For instance, if he meets his son Happy while in the midst of some memory in which Happy disappointed him, he is instantly furious at Happy, despite the fact that Happy at this particular moment deeply desires to be of use to him. He is literally at that terrible moment when the voice of the past is no longer distant but quite as loud as the voice of the present. In dramatic terms the form, therefore, *is* this process, instead of being a once-removed summation or indication of it. (*Collected Works* 25–26)

Willy's Re-lived Memories

Critic Neil Carson points out that "Willy's memories do not materialize at random. They are triggered by certain incidents in the present, and Willy is changed by remembering them." (Carson 48) The lapses fall into two categories. The first consists of mainly happy memories Willy has of being with his sons in 1928 (when Biff is 13, Happy is 11, and the family car is the Chevy) and in 1932 (when Biff at 17 is a high school football star, Happy at 15 is content to share his brother's glory, and the Chevy has accumulated 82,000 miles). Embedded in these scenes of Willy confidently advising and praising his adoring sons are hints of Willy's flawed thinking and its early effect on both sons, especially Biff. In the second category of memory lapse Willy re-lives the rare occasion when Uncle Ben shows up for a brief visit. These scenes provide glimpses of their shared childhood and an older Willy, vulnerable and insecure, eager for advice and praise from Ben.

Willy informs us of the first time lapse in the play when he describes to Linda his confusion about which car he is driving. The first dramatized lapse occurs when he enters the kitchen at Linda's suggestion to make himself a sandwich with something called "whipped cheese." This lapse—signaled by a profusion of leaves that blocks out sight of the apartment buildings—is, according to Carson:

> ... the result of his recollection of the time when Biff seemed so full of promise. It is brought on by Biff's return home and the inevitable tension between the two men which is the consequence of Biff's apparent inability to settle down. It begins with Willy remembering his son waxing the car and proceeds to recollections of other details such as the way in which Biff 'borrowed' a football.... The guilt Willy felt even then about exaggerating his own accomplishments and encouraging his sons to disregard the law is suggested by the appearance of Linda.... Since Willy could never deceive his wife with quite the same facility that he could impress his sons, Linda serves as a kind of conscience making him confess his true earnings and his real sense of inadequacy.... The temporary feeling of intimacy ... reminds Willy that he has not even been honest with Linda, and he attempts to justify his infidelity ... [but] the image of the woman ... [reminds him that] in some ways, he has been more generous to his mistress than to his wife. (Carson 48–49)

Willy in these scenes is quick-tempered and impetuous but he is not exhausted or defeated. High energy and feelings of hope and camaraderie dominate. For Willy in his present anguish, these re-lived episodes with youthful Biff and Happy bring a comforting happiness but they also contain subtle signs of his desperation even back then and intimations that life will not turn out as he euphorically envisions it. These signs of impending trouble are easy for all to ignore at the time because they are obscured by Willy's bravado and high hopes. Watching how and when these memories reassert themselves into his present mental state gives one the sense that Willy's subconscious mind is trying to get his attention not merely to bring comfort but to offer—if not solutions to the present crisis—some clues for understanding it.

We see, for example, in Willy's unlikely stories about having coffee with the mayor of Providence and boasting about receiving personal police protection for his car, his deep-seated need for recognition and his inclination to exaggerate to the point of self-deception. As Carson has noted, even then he was overstating his earnings until gently coaxed to tell the truth by his patient and forgiving wife.

Similarly troubling is the display of what is now commonly referred to as "American exceptionalism"—the presumption of individual entitlement that permits those afflicted with this attitude to think they can ignore with impunity (and often do) established rules and customs. Willy rationalizes Biff's "borrowing" of the regulation football and apparently overlooks his driving without a license. Later, we see Willy praising his sons for stealing lumber from a nearby construction site. Willy proudly calls them "a couple of fearless characters" and Ben agrees, but realistic Charley warns, "... the jails are full of fearless characters."

Biff in these early scenes is in fact a promising young man, physically attractive and gifted with genuine athletic talent. At the same time, it is difficult not to fear that Willy's complacency about bending the rules and his insistence on Biff's special status ("If somebody else took that ball there'd be an uproar.") might produce in Biff an unrealistic—if not dangerously inflated—self-assessment. Biff must also endure his father's volatile moods, experiencing first his worshipful indulgence and then his angry eagerness to "whip" him into proper behavior. "Good behavior" for Biff includes doing well in school but Bernard's tone of alarm about Biff's need to rely on his own work instead of cheating with Bernard's help or— Willy's solution—on his "very likable" personality, resonates with increasing legitimacy as the play proceeds.

As these fragments of the past themselves move through time they become darker and more explicitly ominous. It becomes clear that Willy suffered as a young man from mood swings and an almost unconscious and certainly bizarre habit of self-contradiction. He moves in a single fragment of conversation with Linda from an almost belligerent self-confidence ("Oh, I'll knock 'em dead next week. I'll go to Hartford. I'm very well liked in Hartford.") to a subdued admission of self-doubt ("You know, the trouble is, Linda, people don't seem to take to me."). Moments after joking about making jokes with prospective buyers, he describes an incident in which he imagined himself teased to which he responded precipitously and, apparently, violently. If Willy actually "cracked" the offending person "right across the face" as he states, one wonders why he was not arrested for assault or fired. Accurate or not, the incident is an early sign of a highly unstable and vulnerable personality.

The episode ends with a more explosive manifestation of Willy's mental distress. He has just reaffirmed his love for Linda and his loneliness without her on the road when an unidentified woman's voice makes a disturbing intrusion into their confessional moment. Willy's guilt-ridden mind has summoned her. This jarring and instructive scene of Willy receiving reassurances about his prowess and appeal simultaneously from two women—one thanking him for stockings, the other having to mend her own torn pair—could not have been so memorably dramatized without Miller's innovative treatment of time and stage design.

Willy's Brief Interlude in the Present

Agitated and depleted by the emotional energy of his memories, Willy returns "wilting and staring" to the chronological present and finds himself with Happy who has come down to the kitchen to rescue his father. Biff remains upstairs, immobilized by what he has heard. Happy's intervention consists mainly of glib reassurances which Willy rightly scorns as unrealistic. Later in the scene Happy will attempt to cheer his mother by announcing that he'll soon be getting married—a claim he is even less likely to follow up on than his promise to retire his father for life; and Linda, also realistic, knows it. "Go to bed, dear," she tells him. Happy is well-meaning (he has paid for Willy's respite in Florida) but thoroughly superficial in his response to life's contradiction and dilemmas. His easy answers bring on one of Willy's frightful outbursts: "The woods are burning!"

The guilt and sense of failure generated by this memory lapse prompts Willy into making protestations to Happy of his innocence ("I never ... told him anything but decent things.") and excuses for his life. It is Willy's need for excuses that brings mention of Ben into the play: if only he'd followed Ben's advice to get rich in Alaska! Willy describes Ben with clichés of American Dream rhetoric ("... that man was success incarnate! ... [He] knew what he wanted and went out and got it!"). Then, in this manic moment, he makes one of his curious comments, this one about not cracking open an oyster on a mattress. This gem of cautionary advice is almost certainly a platitude of the times (although it might be Willy's way of declaring that everyone besides himself and Ben, including Happy, is lazy). Either way, the comment illustrates Willy's "commonness," his fervent but unimaginative speech. It is certainly not a reference to himself; Willy is admirably hard-working.

Happy leaves as Charley, having overheard the commotion, walks in the door. Charley offers comfort, distraction, even a job (which prideful Willy rejects). Although scenes with Charley provide humorous diversions in the play, the banter between the two old friends exposes Charley's tolerant and placid nature and Willy's mercurial one. Willy is surprisingly combative and condescending with Charley. Beneath their genuine neighborliness is Willy's unacknowledged envy and anger toward a man like himself who has succeeded in the business world. But Charley lacks the energy and aspiration that animate Willy and attract audience sympathy to him. Charley is content to not care, even suggesting that Willy treat his sons with a little benign forgetting. Willy's indignant and plaintive response ("Then what have I got to remember?") suggests both the impoverishment of his current life without the boys at home but also a certain generosity, a willingness to extend his paternal responsibility—even if guilt-driven—and accept the painful conditions of love and loss. These qualities in Willy contribute to his fatal anguish but they are also appealing, even honorable. It is his life and death that break audience hearts, not Charley's.

Willy's Re-lived Memory with Ben

Willy's dismissal of Charley for not being a man "who can handle [his] tools" brings up a hallucinatory Ben who enters their conversation over cards. Briefly, Willy converses with both men until Charley, baffled and badgered, and too entangled in Willy's mental confusion, loses patience and departs in exasperation.

Without distractions, Willy now falls deeply into a second lapse which yields instructive insight about his earlier life. This remarkable memory reveals that Willy's family of origin was as dysfunctional as it was exciting. Uncle Ben—a "larger-than-life" figure with a blindfolded focus on having staggering amounts of wealth and power—apparently never included his brother's family on his extensive travel routes. Ben doesn't even know their mother has died (he calls her a "fine specimen of a lady") and neither son knows what became of their adventuring father beyond the day he walked out on all of them.

Ben's arrival sends Willy into a long reverie about his first years of life. In this recollection by a mind of its own memories, we learn that Ben and Willy were raised in the ethos of the frontier. This ethos is the mythical center of the American Dream. Lived with integrity and idealism, frontier life demanded physical courage, mental initiative, high spirits, and sustained resolve in order to survive. Ben recalls for Willy their inventive and romantic father: this "very great and very wild-hearted man ... [would] start in Boston ... toss the whole family into the wagon and drive the team right across the country...." It is easy to speculate that these early happy associations with family trips likely influenced Willy's decision to become a traveling salesman. His references to opening up new territories ("[Before] I went north ... the Wagner Company didn't know where New England was!") reinforce the idea that young Willy, imbued with the frontier spirit but also abandoned by a father more devoted to having his own adventures than to responsibly raising his family, may have chosen traveling (*not* selling) for a career to replicate a similar excitement and direction in his adult life but also to symbolically recover the lost father. Willy's excessive and impassioned involvement in his own sons makes more sense in this context as does his tendency to be reckless about the law when it comes to finding building materials for his home. One recalls Willy's early enthusiasm for his car and trips to unfamiliar territories that made for exciting stories for his boys upon his return. But his actual journeys to New England were—by contrast and even at their best—only "wild-hearted" in a tawdry affair and have become, increasingly, occasions for frustration and failure.

Frontier life inspired the best in a person and also—notoriously—the worst. Willy seems not to have noticed the obvious signs of belligerence and corruption in Ben; no doubt because he is blinded by the way his brother has combined wealth with outdoor ruggedness and exotic travel. Ben's flaunting comments (which he repeats like a commercial for himself) about going into the jungle and emerging with so much dazzling wealth—he doesn't even keep accounts of it—never include any practical information about how he did it. (Years later, Willy and Happy are still wondering.) Interestingly, Ben is always in a hurry, as if fearful of something catching up to him.

Ben is an icon of success, the man who makes people believe those tales about pots of gold near rainbows and dollar bills growing on trees. Generations, including that of Willy's father, swarmed across the prairie searching for easy riches. But watching Ben's interactions with his nephews is instructive.

Corruption is at the center of his bravado. Ben applauds the boys' not-so-petty theft of building supplies ("Nervy boy. Good!") and after challenging Biff to a fistfight knocks him ignominiously to the ground with the advice: "Never fight fair with a stranger, boy. You'll never get out of the jungle that way." Linda sensibly asks why Biff needs to be fighting at all; she is, in general, unimpressed by Ben, even resentful. By contrast, in Ben's presence, Willy becomes almost manic. He scornfully dismisses Linda's concerns. He brags to Ben that Biff is capable of chopping down the big trees whose actual destruction by the construction companies he will soon bitterly lament. And he gives a mixed message with the power to confuse and disable otherwise promising young men: he praises his sons for their "fearless" acts of theft and then "[gives] them hell" [for it].

Speculations about Willy in the Past and the Present

Did Willy half-believe his boys were frontiersmen so "special" and "fearless" as to be beyond the law? And with Ben's example and Willy's affirmation of it, did the boys grow up thinking they could get something for nothing, or, if not nothing, then with personal likeableness and Ben's questionable ethics? Has Willy confused his father's frontier spirit with the skills for success in the business world? These are not questions that Miller asks; they are questions that Miller imagines Willy's subconscious mind bringing to consciousness while he struggles mightily to keep disintegration and self-destruction at bay.

Willy's questions are—in important and still relevant ways—real questions for others besides Willy. Frontier life was alluring; Willy's father was appealing. He was adventuresome and hard-working. Also an inventor and artisan: with his own hands he carved flutes that he sold to support the family. His success made possible a wandering lifestyle, one not bound by buildings or other people's schedules, one not like the life Biff bitterly characterizes as "a measly manner of existence." The flute music that accompanies Willy connects him with his father and is not ominous or oppressive. It is genuinely lyrical, innocent and reassuringly simple, evocative of a different way of life. Perhaps Biff's inclination to whistle in elevators—that whimsical act ridiculed by Happy for being inappropriate behavior for anyone interested in "making it" in the business world—connects Biff unconsciously with his grandfather's flutes. Perhaps one explanation for the terrible tension between father and son is that they are more alike than different: animated by a similar spirit (originating for both in Willy's father) but choosing to follow separate and incompatible paths that lead each to frustration and despair. Clearly both have been profoundly affected by the loss of connection to the earth and open spaces. It is the tie that binds both to their lineage and national heritage. Are they animated by wrong ideas? Are their expectations outdated? Should they or anyone relinquish connection to the land in exchange for material success? Although the frontier was mostly gone by 1949, manifestations of national nostalgia for our pioneer past have always been ubiquitous.

By the end of Willy's memory of Ben's visit, it is clear that Ben has significance for Willy far more elemental than his aura of success. In Ben's presence, Willy is beside himself with fluctuating needs and emotions. Fatherless himself, Willy looks to his older brother for advice and confirmation while he ardently tries to impress him with his boys' manliness and half-true references to his own success. Ben's response is erratic and never helpful. He cavalierly praises the boys' antics but diminishes Willy with his condescension: "And good luck with your—what do you do?" Confronted by Willy's explicit request for more of his company, Ben imperiously responds: "I'll stop by on my way back to Africa." And to Willy's brave and revealing confession ("... I still feel kind of temporary about myself.") Ben can only come up with: "I'll be late for my train." Ben's visit is fundamentally unsatisfying and unproductive yet Willy's need for him is both tenacious and inexhaustible.

Commenting on the instructive insights provided by Willy's lapses into the past, Benjamin Nelson makes two helpful points. He writes in *Arthur Miller: Portrait of a Playwright,*

"This series of episodes, which centers on Willy and his sons, shows the father trying to substantiate his ecstatic belief in the success ideal [of the American Dream] by superimposing it upon his children." (Nelson 109) Later he sums up: "Ultimately each event dredged out of his past makes the same point about Willy Loman: his life is caught in an unresolvable dichotomy between fact and fancy. He is unable to separate his individuality from his conception of himself as a supersalesman because he cannot truly differentiate between the two." (Nelson 109–110) Such elementary incoherence about identity is a likely consequence of being abandoned by a mythical father. Ben cannot and will not satisfy this need for a father. In Neil Carson's words, "Willy's problems as a father are shown to be a direct result of his deprivation as a son, and it is part of the richness of *Death of a Salesman* that its perspective encompasses three generations." (Carson 50)

Conclusion of Act One

In a 1995 interview for BBC radio Miller described the average person's experience of living through the Depression. He used images that are relevant for anyone living at the outer edges of economic or emotional survival: "... [There] is a feeling at the back of the brain that the whole thing can sink at a moment's notice ... everything else is ephemeral. It is going to blow away, except what a person is and what a relationship is." (Bigsby, ed. 1) In the concluding scene of Act One Willy has returned to the chronological present. All four family members are under the same roof for what will be their last night as a whole family. For different reasons, Willy, Linda, and Biff—each one in isolation—are experiencing that "feeling at the back of the brain."

When Linda answers Biff's question about what to do about Willy's bizarre behavior—"Oh, my dear, you should do a lot of things, but there's nothing to do, so go to sleep"—we hear the exhaustion of her day-to-day effort to keep Willy together. When she says "I live from day to day"—we hear her dread that "the whole thing can sink at a moment's notice."

Thomas Porter describes Willy's state of mind in this way:

When [Willy] momentarily faces reality—his inability to drive to Boston, the mounting bills and the dwindling income—he has to flee to the past and to project the future. The salesman cannot abandon the myth [of success] without reducing himself to zero. Thus, he must hope. (Porter 137)

For Willy this means projecting his hope onto Biff. For Biff it means carrying the burden of Willy's hopes. To save his father Biff must take on a filial task that threatens his own survival and the reconciliation between father and son that both urgently need. Linda, at the edge of her strength, makes Biff's task explicit. In the tense scene with her sons when she discloses the evidence that Willy's "accidents" are suicide attempts, she tells Biff: "... I swear to God! Biff, his life is in your hands!" Beneath all fears and doubts is the need for right relationship with oneself and others: "... everything ... is ephemeral.... except what a person is and what a relationship is." With this view in mind, the play can be understood as a drama less about failing dreams and more about the importance of the ties that bind. This is the substance of Linda's famous "Attention must be paid" speech. Although addressed to her sons about their exhausted father, its language suggests a voice with more authority, as if it were a commandment being delivered authoritatively to a wider audience. Attention, it seems to be saying, must be paid to every person.

By the time Willy returns from his walk to see the stars, his sons have fully grasped the extremity of the family crisis. Linda's speech has worked. Biff and Happy have vowed to change their ways. For Biff it entails a radical change.

Biff's Crisis

Biff has come home because he is tormented by a need to understand himself, to know "what a person is." At 34, he is, in his own words, still "just ... a boy," unable to marry or find satisfying work. By coming home to confront the past Biff is following an ageless pattern. He knows the pervasive irresolution in his life is tied to his relationship with his father.

Late in the play, during their tumultuous final encounter, Biff will furiously accuse his father of fostering a delusional sense of entitlement—an assumption that all doors will automatically open on his path to success: "... I never got anywhere because you blew me so full of hot air that I could never stand taking orders from anybody!"

Linda understands one aspect of Biff's dilemma ("Biff, a man is not a bird, to come and go with the springtime.") but she has no inkling of the secret he has been carrying for years about Willy's infidelity to her. The harm to Biff from carrying so virulent a secret is detected in his cynical dismissal of Happy's naïve assumptions and his sudden apprehension at the mention of "a woman." The nature of the secret precipitates an early fall from innocence for Biff; it was a transfiguring event with reverberating consequences. The fleeting eruption of "the woman" out of Willy's unconscious into his conscious memory just moments earlier is a sign of her importance to Willy for his story about himself and the tormenting guilt she continues to represent. The secret shared by Biff and Willy binds them in an emotional firestorm. In this context, Biff's offer to stay home, get a job, and support his parents is a painful sacrifice of a dutiful son but it is a bizarre sacrifice—and almost doomed not to succeed—because Biff is an adult and has more appropriate tasks to perform. Making this commitment also provides Biff with a clear and urgent focus, a temporary way out of his own tormenting confusion. Nonetheless, Biff's gesture—however obviously it rises out of alarm and a misdirected effort at self-rescue—seems also to be motivated by a son's genuine love for his father.

The Family's Crisis

In his introduction to *Arthur Miller: A Collection of Critical Essays*, Robert W. Corrigan makes an interesting assessment of Miller and his main characters by applying the categories of human development put forward by Erik Erikson. Erikson (in *Identity and the life cycle*, 1959) describes eight stages of growth, each with a defining crisis. The crises of Identity, Generativity, and Integrity are acutely relevant to Willy and Biff. Identity formation is the struggle of late adolescence and early adulthood; generativity follows in middle age at the peak of ones productivity in society; and integrity is the achievement of perspective and self-acceptance in old age. Corrigan points out that several of Miller's adult characters including Willy are still suffering with unresolved identity crises. He observes that the death of each of these characters was brought on by an absence of self-understanding:

> ... this blindness is ... due to their failure to have resolved the question of identity at an earlier and more appropriate time in life. Miller presents this crisis as a conflict between the uncomprehending self and a solid social or economic structure—the family, the community, the system. The drama emerges either when the protagonist breaks his connection with society or when unexpected pressures reveal that such a connection has in fact never even existed. Miller sees the need for such a connection as absolute, and the failure to achieve and/or maintain it is bound to result in catastrophe. (Corrigan 2–3)

One recalls here Willy's remark about feeling "temporary" and his unreflective allegiance to incompatible ideas about how to live and succeed. The salesman's business ethic dictates behavior that would endanger life on the frontier; the qualifications for survival on the frontier would likely land a businessman in jail; and Willy's own confused notions about winning success by being "likeable" are insufficient for achieving success of any kind. Conducting a life according to ideals that work for separate and different paradigms has left Willy bewildered and profoundly unsatisfied with his life. One remedy for dealing with the complex challenges encountered in life is reflection followed by awareness leading to informed choices that constitute a productive and satisfying identity. But Willy belongs to a class and a profession that does not foster (and might even discourage) self-understanding. Deprived of a father and lacking incentives and capacity for self-awareness, Willy had multiple reasons—even before he entered the salesman's unpredictable world—to feel "temporary about [himself]." His identity confusion has persisted into his older age creating instability for the whole family and catastrophe for him and Biff.

For years Willy has been looking at Biff as an extension of himself, the bearer of his hope for the future. His disordered thinking likely originated at the 1932 Ebbets Field game when he effectively stopped time at the moment Biff in his eyes arrived at the height of his youthful glory and was still exuding great promise. Willy felt himself implicated in Biff's glory; he remembers the crowd calling out the name "Loman, Loman, Loman!" His psychological need to stop time at this juncture of Biff's life was not understood at the time nor was it ever acknowledged later in the family. Such a desperate act of hubris committed by one family member ineluctably affects the other members though perhaps in less acute and more disguised ways. The impairment of family functioning and integrity— although its underlying causes are at this point in the play as yet unacknowledged and unarticulated—has been of long duration. Linda has confused her wife and mother roles: she warns her 63-year-old husband to "be careful on the stairs" and appears to be turning all her anger on her sons. Certainly, Happy has not become a responsible adult. He admits to his own identity confusion ("I don't know what the hell I'm workin' for.") and his self-serving ethics are typical of one who suffers from deep insecurities. Linda calls him "a philandering bum" and he seems to be one reckless step away from being found out. Interestingly, Linda reveals nothing about her life other than her efforts to save Willy's.

As for Biff, this frozen-in-time version of himself transcends the need for identity formation. Even language cannot define him: he was, in Willy's enraptured words, "[like] a young god. Hercules ... something like that." Now that Willy has endured the ignominious loss of what stature and identity he had achieved—"... they [took] his salary away ... he's been on straight commission"—he is, in Linda's words "... a beginner, an unknown" and his sense of deprivation has become life-threatening. Willy cannot rest until Biff has achieved something commensurate with the larger-than-life image he has imposed on his son. And Biff's crisis will remain acute until he discovers and affirms who he is that is not merely Willy's dream, and he will need Willy's confirmation that he has done so. A family closer to breakdown than the Loman family at the end of Act One would be hard to imagine.

The final hours of family life depicted at the end of Act One are dominated by emotional extremes—dread, rage, euphoria—and sudden reversals into their opposites. When Willy learns that Biff has agreed to ask his old boss Bill Oliver for help starting a business of his own, he erupts into euphoria unrestrained by any realistic considerations. One of these considerations is the fact that Biff was a mere shipping clerk for Oliver, not one of his salesmen, and he stole basketballs from the store. Again Willy exaggerates, his hopeful imagination racing ahead to unlikely outcomes. Of course Biff will go into sporting goods! Of course he will succeed because "[he knows] sporting goods better than Spaulding, for God's sake!" And he sees money in Biff's hand before Biff has seen Oliver. When reminded of this obvious fact, he instantly punctures all hopes and sinks into his familiar despondency. Within a matter of seconds Biff goes from hearing Willy's excessive praise to hearing his unjustified scorn: "Ah, you're counting your chickens again." We can assume that Biff has endured countless similar experiences of his father's mercurial nature. Happy—caught up in the family need for optimism—proposes a partnership with Biff—"The Loman Brothers"—which Willy instantly pronounces "a one-million-dollar idea!" Thomas Porter comments:

> This scene is generated out of the heart of myth. 'Loman Brothers' has, for Willy and the boys, the ring of personality and solidarity and achievement. It would not entail entering the impersonal arena of the office; the boys' would be 'out playin' ball again.' With no regular hours to cramp their freedom and no fierce outside competition, there would be the 'old honor and comradeship.' Sportsmanship, clean living, economic

freedom would blend in a million-dollar enterprise, the ideal life crowned with financial achievement. Only the glowing pair who ran to carry their father's valises and to listen to his prideful predictions would consider such a scheme 'talking sense.' (Porter 140)

The family member likely to feel doubt at this precarious family juncture is Linda and she has important reservations which—a bit diffidently—she tries to make known. But she has, in Benjamin Nelson's words, "helped build a doll's house around [Willy who] has been doing [the same thing] to Biff and Happy." (Nelson 112) Of course, she, too, wants to hope and it makes sense that she chooses to tread lightly. In any case, Willy is under too much pressure from his relentless inner agenda to even notice her. Almost obsessively, he interrupts her and dismisses all her interventions except those that bring him immediate comfort. At this point in his disintegration he can only hear reassuring words, only bear to consider a single outcome. "I see great things for you kids," Willy declares, "I think your troubles are over." And his, as well. Willy is determined to see his boss the next morning to ask for the less strenuous job of non-traveling salesman. Act One concludes as each family member summons the resources and courage needed to make the next day work out as planned, and the family makes a collective effort to rescue itself and prevail.

Act Two

The second act contains two of the most painful scenes in Western literature. It is now morning. Although Willy has slept—ominously—"like a dead one," music "bright and gay" introduces the scene setting up a parallel between the happy adventuring of Willy's original family and the hopeful ventures to the wilderness of the business world that Willy and Biff are undertaking today. The nostalgic spell cast by the shaving lotion fragrance left by the departing sons kindles in Willy and Linda a new level of high expectations. The father will confront his current boss and the son will visit his old boss— both hoping their separate encounters will yield the same result: a life-saving hold on a new life. Willy is— characteristically—swept up by his "fast-track" optimism but on this morning he outdoes himself with visions of moving with Linda to a "little place out in the country" with room for chickens and a garden. Matthew Roudané calls this Willy's "inability to observe his own emotional speed limits." (Bigsby, ed. 79)

Although hints of Linda's complicity with Willy's illusions have been heard earlier in her encouraging assurances that he is "doing fine" and "will do better next week," these remarks can also be understood as the normal support a wife would give a husband in discouraging times. This morning, however, she seems to have thrown out her reservations and joined the illusion. "Handsome" Biff, for example, "could be a—anything" dressed in his blue suit. When she announces that he'd left earlier in a hopeful mood and "couldn't wait to get downtown to see Oliver," we wonder if she is telling the truth or imagining this change of heart because that change is essential for her husband's survival. Biff did make a commitment to the family the night before, but only an hour earlier he had bitterly called "a measly manner of existence" the life he is now pursuing. Miller is also careful to note that Biff goes to sleep barely able to be in his father's presence. Everything that has happened in the past is still with them. Linda's mood, in fact, suddenly deflates when she learns that Biff, not Willy, has removed the rubber tube connecting.

An important function of this morning scene is to establish for the audience a sense of commonality with Willy. When Linda mentions the car and refrigerator bills, we ask: Who has not dealt with mortgages, time payments, and "grace periods?" Who has not been deluded by clever advertising? Who has not felt anger when machines and gadgets malfunction, when appliances break down before one is finished paying for them? Who has not felt "temporary" at some time or been fearful of not "making it.?" When Willy says "I'm always in a race with the junkyard!" he may be referring unconsciously to his own fate but he is also speaking the truth for all of us. When he accuses manufacturers of "[timing] those things so when you finally [pay] for them, they're used up," we share his cynicism and it is justified. Miller was convinced that we all "knew Willy." At the deepest level all human beings need hope to keep going. And many many people are animated by hopes that are as unlikely to come about as Willy's are. Willy's hopefulness is not why he fails. When he walks out the door on the way to see Howard he carries expectations that are not unreasonable.

The Meeting with Howard

Willy's meeting with Howard is a pivotal scene in the play. Willy finds Howard in his office fiddling with a tape recorder, recently invented and typical of the mechanical gadgets that were quickly proliferating in the postwar economy. Howard is so mesmerized by the intricacies of his new possession that he does not notice that Willy is supposed to be on the road today. Nor is he aware of Willy's need or mission. For several minutes Willy functions as Howard's audience, an occasion to show off his children's voices that were awkwardly recorded the night before. Remembering that Willy and Linda count pennies to make their payments, it is uncomfortable to watch as he hears Howard's casual reference to the cost ("only a hundred and a half") and offhand assumption that every family has a maid at home to record favorite programs for later listening.

The outcome of the meeting is worse than Willy could have anticipated. Howard first declines to give Willy the job change he has requested and then takes away the job he has. To each effort Willy makes to plead his case—each one diminishing in size and dignity as he grows more desperate—Howard gives the infamous "yes, but" response and refers to him as "kid." His question to Willy—"But where am I going to put you, kid?"—recalls Linda's admonition to Biff earlier in the day: "Be loving to [your father]. Because he's only a little boat looking for a harbor." In all Willy hears eight "buts" in a 30-second conversation that concludes with Howard's remark: "Well, you gotta admit, business is business." Willy has no place, no safe harbor, no room for a garden, and now no job. In the economic system Willy belongs to, having no job is equivalent to having no identity.

The scene of Howard firing Willy created controversy for Miller. At one extreme is Eleanor Clark's commentary accusing Miller of creating an "intellectual muddle" by compromising ideology with attempts to make Willy's fate universally relevant. She writes:

> It is, of course, the capitalist system that has done Willy in; the scene in which he is brutally fired after some forty years with the firm comes straight from the party-line literature of the thirties, and the idea emerges lucidly enough through all the confused motivations of the play that it is our particular form of money economy that has bred the absurdly false ideals of both father and sons. (Welland 52)

Raymond Williams in a passage cited earlier sees a system in which loyal participants like Willy slowly become commodities themselves which in turn become outmoded and discarded. Some critics who praised the play for its ideology criticized Miller for not going far enough. Samuel Siller, writing in 1949 for *Masses & Mainstream*, felt Miller had undermined his own point by including a benign capitalist in the figure of Charley. And playwright Lorraine Hansberry sees Willy as emblematic of the irony at the center of the American dream:

> a nation of great military strength, indescribable material wealth, and incredible mastery of the physical realm [is] unable ... to produce a typical hero who [is] capable of an affirmative view of life.... Something has indeed gone wrong with at least past of the American Dream, and Willy Loman is the victim of the detour. (Hansberry 7)

Other critics point out that Willy's numerous personal flaws precipitate his own downfall. They cite evidence for Willy's moral laxity with his sons, his self-deceptions, his reactive personality, and, most directly relevant, his ineffectual efforts to make enough sales to justify ongoing service to the firm. Critic Arthur Gantz argues that Willy was simply a foolish man who wrongly believed that "success in the business world [could] be achieved not by work and ability but by being 'well-liked,' by a kind of hearty popularity that [would] open all doors and provide favors and preferential treatment." (Gantz 125–28) Gantz points out that after Howard reminds Willy that "business is business" Willy says he agrees but behaves as if he does not. Against Howard's objections, Willy offers a story about the legendary Dave Singleman which is subjectively— but not objectively—relevant and Willy does not recognize the difference.

Paula Marantz Cohen takes an approach which makes considerations of ideology less relevant. In her essay "Why is Willy confused?" Cohen suggests reading *Death of a Salesman* with a focus on the paradigm shift beginning to take place at the historical time of the play. The transition from labor and machine productivity to intellectual and technical power restructures the methods of communication that organize a society. In this context she sees Willy's traveling salesman job as sharing the one-way extractive mentality of the pioneers: set your goal, make your sales pitch, take what you can get and move on. Interestingly, she sees Willy's style of selling through being a likeable and engaging personality more useful for an age when most people have discretionary money and are more likely to make purchase choices based on personal associations. She writes:

> Significantly, it is Howard who introduces the single symbol of the new in the play.... [The tape recorder] is a device that is mechanical without being productive in any obvious sense. It doesn't make anything but noise and, when not mobilized for communication purposes, it seems a childish indulgence. Yet the machine is meaningful in a historical context. It symbolizes the beginning of a new wave of communication devices for business use.... Miller provides us with a clue [to the machine's future usefulness] in the figure of Bernard, the play's representative of the future. Bernard is in the field of communication; he is a litigator, and his profession is

destined to play a powerful role in the coming information society.... (Roudané, ed. 128)

Cohen speculates that the outcome in Howard's office might have been different had Willy asked "Did your father ever tell you ...?" instead of "Your father came to me the day you were born...." Delivered this way, the statement allows no room for a response. It is packaged sentiment and seems drawn out of the very salesman's kit that can no longer sell the buyers in New England. Willy ends up selling himself out of a job because his plea brings home to his employer, if only subliminally, the ineffectiveness of the old-style salesmanship with its reliance on one-way communication. (Roudané, ed. 128) She praises Miller for what she regards as his "intuitive grasp of the direction of his society's evolution." (126)

Critic Ronald Hayman does not comment directly on Willy's being fired but reminds us that the claustrophobia that Willy expresses when speaking of his home "is linked with the mechanization and urbanization [of his time] and [his] madness is linked with a nostalgia for the better times in the past." (Hayman 30) When Willy cannot control the tape-recorder after Howard has left the room he responds hysterically like one both mad and claustrophobic. Similarly, Matthew Roudané suggests that Willy's response to Howard's machine is "a symbolic reminder of how far Willy lags behind his own technological era...."

[When the machine] talks to Willy [he] has no idea of how to turn off the new-fangled invention. The taped voice of Howard's son spinning out of control foregrounds, of course, Willy's own life, which is spinning out of control. After all, Willy does not fit in with the industrialized world; he is more at home in a pastoral world, one in which he can use his hands to build a porch or plant seed in a garden. (Bigsby, ed. 76)

Critic Dennis Welland in his book on Miller reviews some of the differing interpretations of Howard's treatment of Willy and concludes: "The evidence for a Marxist interpretation of *Death of a Salesman* is ... not very impressive. The scene [of Willy's firing] is theatrically ... moving [and] painful ... but it engenders a mixture of pity and exasperation rather than the indignation that we would expect of a 'party-line' literature...." (Welland 54) Welland joins other critics in noting the presence of successful-but-also-kindly Charley as a contrast to Howard. Welland attributes Howard's dismissal of Willy to his self-absorption:

> The tape-recorder scene serves two purposes in the scene: when Willy ... sets it accidentally in motion it precipitates a hysterical breakdown that symbolizes the central theme of the play in Willy's horror at his inability to switch it off—to switch off the recorded past. Whether the past is that of his own sons recorded on his memory and conscience, or that of Howard's son recorded on a mechanical instrument, it is the past, more than capitalism, of which Willy is always the victim.... The machine also [dramatizes] Howard's ingenuous pride in his children. They are far more real to him than is the memory of his father to which Willy constantly appeals, and his pride in their prowess and their affection for him obliterates any understanding of Willy's plight, exactly as Willy's pride in his sons has blinded him to any recognition of the worth of Bernard. (54)

Although artists do not control the range of meanings their works may reflect, Miller has been unusually accessible to his audiences and it is always illuminating to hear him speak about his intentions. His comments about producing *Death of a Salesman* in China are especially useful because he was challenged to explain himself to actors unacquainted with American ideas. He had also been thinking about his most famous character for 34 years. Miller instructed the actor playing Howard: "... Willy is trying to tell you ... that the impersonality of business is destroying him.... Your answer is that you are helpless to do anything for him, you are both caught in the same machine." (*"Salesman" in Beijing* 135) He then converses with the other actors about the transition in China from socialist theory that emphasizes cooperation between people to the recent commercialization of life where, increasingly, specialists are trained and paid for work that used to be done by the community. He concludes that the play "does not have the solution to this problem—the alienation brought by technological advance—because I don't have the solution. What I present is the price we pay for our progress." (136)

This acknowledgement brings criticism from Tom Driver who accuses Miller of "[lacking] that metaphysical inquisitiveness which would have taken him to the bottom of the problems he encounters." He cites the "ambiguity ... in the question of society versus the individual" and asks "[Is the 'law' that Willy breaks] imposed upon him by a white collar industrial society? If so, what is wrong with such a society and what truth does it prevent Willy from seeing?" (Bloom 17)

Similarly, Eric Mottram praises Miller's evocation of the human suffering embodied in Willy but asks: "... if the hero dies at his own hand, with the sense of waste and bewilderment still entire within him, who can now be interested in anything but the chance of changing the ... society that brings him to that degradation?" (Corrigan, ed. 32)

Arthur Miller has been interested in politics since his college years and active over the years in labor and other issues. To this day he speaks out against injustices committed by corporations and governments (including his own). But he is an artist first:

A play cannot be equated with a political philosophy.... I do not believe that any work of art can help but be diminished by its adherence at any cost to a political program, including its author's, and not for any other reason than that there is no political program—any more than there is a theory of tragedy—which can encompass the complexities of real life. Doubtless an author's politics must be one element, and even an important one, in the germination of his art, but if it is art he has created it must by definition bend itself to his observation rather than to his opinions or even his hopes. (*Collected Plays* 36)

Interlude with Ben

Regardless of the role American capitalism played in Willy's fate, Willy himself responds to his mortification with a declaration and a story about his origins. Recalling the inspiration that propelled him into the selling business, he reminds Howard that back then "there was personality in it ... there was respect, and comradeship, and gratitude in it.... [unlike] today [when] it's all cut and dried...." With a minimum of ritual politeness Howard ushers Willy out the door, leaving him with the almost certain false promise that he'll reconsider if Willy goes home and takes a long rest. Failing to recover any stability or peace of mind with his visit to Howard, Willy departs and falls into another memory lapse with Ben. One imagines him here as Miller once described him—a normal-appearing man mumbling to himself—this time on a New York City sidewalk on his way without quite knowing it to Charley's office.

Willy is animated by images of mythical places. In his conversation with Howard, he evokes a plush and comforting image of the salesman's territory that ends with the inspiring funeral of Dave Singleman. Here his unconscious memory has summoned Ben from a mythical frontier, a mythical jungle, because he associates Ben with a pivotal choice he made in the past. Willy punishes himself by persistently wondering how his life would be different had he followed Ben to Alaska.

This episode—like Willy's other memory lapses—is not a reliable source of objective information, only of Willy's selective remembering. To the extent that he accurately recalls Linda in these scenes, we can discern that she had a more active and complex role in Willy's life than earlier scenes have suggested. Linda is not happy to see Ben on this, his second visit to the family. To Ben's alluring description of rugged work in his newly acquired timberland Linda insists, "He's got a beautiful job here [and] is doing well enough...." Ben's condescending answer—"Well enough for what?"—is a real question with much more than Willy's material success implied, although that consideration is in the playwright's mind (and ours), not Ben's. Was moving to Alaska a realistic option for the Loman family? Linda shows no potential for being a happy prairie woman or lumberjack's wife; she seems here to be protecting a stable and secure—if dull and unchallenging—way of life for herself and her family. It is easy to simplify Linda. She is certainly loyal and lovingly supportive to her husband, but when he proclaims with determination "We'll do it here, Ben," meaning staying in Brooklyn, has he allowed her to take away something vital in him? We recall that Willy was raised by his mother after his father deserted the family. Without paternal direction in his life, Willy may have become too accustomed to female influence. This scene may raise questions of blame, more interesting but perhaps less useful.

Willy's Meeting with Bernard and Charley

Willy arrives at Charley's office engaged out loud in a remembered conversation that took place on the day of the 1932 Ebbets Field game in which he responds to Charley's teasing with inappropriate combativeness. We see Willy behaving like one "who can't take a joke," adding to the impression gained through earlier hints that he has difficulty with certain kinds of social interactions despite his insistence on being a likeable guy. Willy finds grown-up Bernard whistling to himself in his father's reception room. Clearly Happy is mistaken in his theory of the deleterious effects of whistling because Bernard is stopping to visit his father on his way to argue a case before the Supreme Court. In Bernard's presence Willy's inclination to exaggerate expands to the point of fantasy and his flawed reasoning leads to odd assumptions. He tells Bernard that Bill Oliver has summoned Biff from out west and he is sure that people who have their own tennis courts must be "fine people" when they could just as easily be crooks. Nonetheless, the ensuing scene is the first in the play thus far in which respect, authenticity, and human decency dominate. Willy is gracious about Bernard's accomplishments; Bernard is self-effacing about those same accomplishments and genuinely solicitous with Willy; Charley, once again, offers Willy money, a job, and simple kindness; and Willy is finally truthful about himself and vulnerable with Charley.

This time Charley also gives Willy a clairvoyant and kindly message: "Willy, nobody's worth nothin' dead." There is something grimly inevitable about this chance meeting of Bernard, Charley, and Willy. Willy is a broken man now, clinging to his final hope that for his son Biff the day has gone well. He has arrived at the point in his mental disintegration where nothing remains to be lost and he can endure the most damaging and humiliating of his memories. The mystery is what motivates the return of these memories. Perhaps Willy has simply lost all his defenses. Perhaps the unconscious mind is a cruel tyrant. It is not possible to fathom the workings of the mind. But from this point on in the play—beneath the entire emotional conflagration still to come—there is something noble and certainly poignant in the sight of a despairing soul seeking explanations for his fate. To Bernard's counsel—"... Sometimes, Willy, it is better for a man to just walk away"—Willy replies: "but if you can't walk away?" Miller sees in this incapacity to walk away one mark of a tragic stature. He writes about the moment of commitment in a play, "that moment when, in my eyes, a man differentiates himself from every other man, that moment when out of a sky full of stars he fixes on one star. I take it, as well ... that the less capable a man is of walking away from the central conflict of the play, the closer he approaches a tragic existence." (*Collected Poems* 7)

"*Small and alone*," Willy asks, "What's the secret?" Why did Bernard succeed and Biff fail? He recalls Bernard inquiring about what happened to Biff on his visit to Willy in Boston that seemed to have broken Biff's spirit. Willy makes a final effort to beat back the dreaded memory before leaving to meet his sons at the restaurant.

The Restaurant Scene
If *Death of a Salesman* had been performed for the past 150 years instead of 50, we would know Marx's view of the scene with Howard and Freud's view of the restaurant scene.

Sexuality, betrayal, and the elemental conflict between father and son are all dramatized in this climatic scene. The meeting for dinner at the restaurant—anticipated by each participant as an event of family celebration and communion—is, in fact, an occasion for the enactment of love between family members, but love at its most convoluted and desperate.

Happy arrives first with an air suggesting that he has either forgotten the original purpose of the family dinner or is ready to abandon it in exchange for some tawdry fun with the girls. In every exchange with the waiter and the two girls Happy exposes his vanity, superficiality, and self-promoting aggressiveness. Somehow it is fitting that he makes a point of ordering lobsters with big claws for a dinner no one ever eats. Some critics find this scene unlikely; certainly, it is extreme. In no other scene in the play are the effects of being what Biff will later call being "[blown] full of hot air" so plainly displayed. His flamboyant exaggerations ("Biff is quarterback for the New York Giants") and seductive salesman's talk create a deeply ironic setting for the arrival of Willy and Biff who must disclose to each other the disastrous consequences these attributes may create.

Biff arrives next, ready to tell the truth, desperate to present to his brother and father, especially his father, an authentic version of himself, a story—however humiliating—he can tell with integrity. But Happy, whose stake in Biff's life was minimal until he concocted the "Loman Brothers" fantasy the night before, listens to the story but with less interest in its significance for Biff than in making sure Willy doesn't hear it. "[Tell] him something nice," is Happy's advice. He continues to think it's appropriate to try to fix Biff up with one of the random women in the restaurant. The brothers could not be less alike here. Happy has inherited his Uncle Ben's bravado and extractive mentality. Biff has inherited his grandfather's wanderlust, which he has been struggling to put into a form that will earn his father's approval. Earlier that morning Biff had approached Oliver with the assumption that he would be remembered as a good salesman rather than the shipping clerk who stole a carton of basketballs. The moment when Oliver doesn't recognize Biff is the occasion for Biff to recognize himself for the first time.

At the center of Biff's epiphany is his impulsive theft of Oliver's pen. Superficially a reckless act, it may have served an important unconscious purpose; namely, rescuing Biff from ever having to work for Oliver or anyone like him. In the final confrontation between Biff and his father that occurs later in the evening, Biff describes himself leaving Oliver's office in a way that supports this interpretation:

> I ran down eleven flights with a pen in my hand today. And suddenly I stopped, you hear me? And in the middle of that office building, do you hear this? I stopped in the middle of that building and I saw—the sky. I saw the things I love in this world. The work and the food and the time to sit and smoke. And I looked at the pen and said to myself, what the hell am I grabbing this for? Why, am I trying to become what I don't want to be?

Paula Cohen discusses the issue of stealing in the context of family dynamics:

> Willy fails to see how lessons he has taught at home may take shape in other contexts. In the flashback scenes, Willy thus praises Biff for his initiative in stealing a football and in taking lumber from a nearby site to rebuild the front stoop; later, when an adult Biff confesses to his father that he stole Bill Oliver's pen, Willy will not hear the confession. We see that Biff has become a thief because of the messages he received at home and that home, which should be a source of comfort and forgiveness is precisely the place where his confession can not be heard. (Roudané, ed. 129)

Matthew Roudané expands the notion of theft:

> From Happy's stealing other executives' fiancées to Biff's stealing the high school football, the box full of

basketballs, the lumber and cement from the neighborhood, the suit in Kansas City, and Bill Oliver's fountain pen, the question of stealing deepens to encompass not only social crimes but fundamental issues private issues: the stealing of one's very identity, the loss of the self, the abrogation of responsibility. (Bigsby, ed. 69)

Roudané's view is consistent with the charge against capitalism to the extent that the commercialization of culture robs individuals of their inner nature. It is the sensation of recovering one's inner nature that Biff experiences with Oliver. And the emotional release that follows such a hard-earned moment of truth energizes Biff's behavior in the restaurant. He is ready to be his own man, but neither his brother nor his father will permit it. Biff and Willy have parallel stories to bring to the restaurant, but for several moments after Willy's arrival each can only concentrate on the other's failure. Biff is stunned to learn that Willy has been fired, while Willy attempts to re-invent Biff's story according to the optimistic expectations he has been carrying around all day. Biff, who is newly determined to "hold on to the facts tonight," finds Willy's distortions—and Happy's complicity in them—unbearable, and he seems ready to flee in exasperation rather than stay and join the old family pattern of fixing things by mutual and multiple deceptions. Only after Biff panics at the sight of Willy spinning out of control, frantic with guilt and pain, does he succumb to Happy's advice. "Pop, listen!" he beseeches, "Listen to me! I'm telling you something good," and then lies about Oliver responding to their "Loman Brothers" scheme.

Biff cannot sustain this deception. The truth comes out anyway and Willy is utterly undone by it. He is seized by the memory of hiding his mistress in the hotel washroom. Staggering out of his chair Willy stumbles toward the restaurant restroom where he sinks into a re-enactment of his most dreaded memory: Biff's discovery of his infidelity to Linda. Remarkably, Happy is mainly concerned here with restoring the impression he had earlier made on Miss Forsythe, who has gone off to fetch a date for Biff. Happy is misguided in his priorities, while Biff, who needs to flee from this terrible scene, takes a stand before he leaves. Resentful of the inappropriate intrusion of Happy's women into a critical and plainly private family episode, Biff announces with great feeling: "Miss Forsythe, you've just seen a prince walk by. A fine troubled prince. A hard-working, unappreciated prince. A pal, you understand? A good companion. Always for his boys." A moment later, Happy will betray this "prince [who was] always for his boys" by denying that Willy is his father. "He's just a guy," he tells the women as they depart together, abandoning Willy in the restroom.

The Woman

While Biff is telling the world, in effect, that his father is a "prince," Willy is in the throes of his nightmarish memory in which this same son called him "[A] fake! [A] phony little fake!" Biff's discovery of his father's infidelity takes place in the summer of 1932—a few months after his victorious game at Ebbets Field. Within a year Biff provides his father with his moment of greatest glory and moment of greatest shame. Despite Bernard's help, Biff has failed math by four points and won't be able to attend college as planned. Knowing he can count on his father, Biff makes a surprise trip to Boston where Willy is on a sales trip. Biff's discovery of Willy's mistress in his hotel room—his witness to a perversion of the primal scene—reminds critic Leonard Moss of the ancient family drama involving what Shakespeare in *King Lear* called 'unnaturalness between child and the parent'—'the bond crack'd 'twixt son and father':

> *Death of a Salesman* ... repeats that archetypal plot in which a son ... looks to his father for moral direction ... instead finds corruption ... and severs the bond of mutual respect.... [This] breach of trust, shame and resentment prevent permanent reunion.... Biff ... suffers an emotional and moral shock experienced by numerous other literary figures, including the biblical Adam.... He begins in security and innocence; proceeds through enlightenment,

indignation, disillusion, and despair; and ends in cynical, sorrowful resignation. (Moss 24-25)

Matthew Roudané focuses on Willy in this scene:

Miller fills the daydream scene in Boston with images of a fall, moving from the chair at Frank's Chop House to the bed in the Standish Arms.... [where Willy has fallen into bed with The Woman.] After hearing Biff's knocking on the door, she pleads , 'Willy, ... are you going to get up, get up, get up, get up?' while the audience watches a man in the process of falling down, down, down, down. (Bigsby, ed. 67)

In this scene Miller makes Biff's struggle equal to Willy's struggle. How is a son to behave when the father he admires and is ready to emulate has also been the occasion for irrevocable disillusionment? Biff, weeping, crumbles before Willy after Willy has banished The Woman from the room. Willy responds with two voices: "She's nothing to me, Biff. I was lonely...."; and, seconds later when Biff, unable to accept his explanation, tries to leave, not reconciled, Willy, aggressively asserts his authority: "I gave you an order." Biff does not obey and leaves Willy alone on the hotel room floor, as he and Happy have just left him alone in the restaurant. We don't see Biff in the months and years that follow this encounter, but we do see the consequences. In the conversation Willy has with Bernard in Charley's office, we learn that Biff disappeared for a month after his trip to Boston, and when he returned he burned his college sneakers, fought with Bernard, and refused to go to summer school where he could have made up the lost credit. "I've often thought," says Bernard, "of how strange it was that I knew he'd given up his life." And then the question that pierces Willy's heart: "What happened in Boston, Willy?" Since the play gives no clues to the contrary, we can assume that Biff has been carrying his secret alone all these years. In family dynamic terms it would be labeled a "toxic secret" and much evidence could be produced showing the virulent effect on the secret-bearer and the insidious effect on the others involved. We do know that in recent years Biff has been unsettled (like "a bird ... [coming] and [going] with the springtime") and we are soon to learn that he's been in jail for a series of petty thefts. It is impossible not to wonder how different Biff's life might have been had Willy had the courage to acknowledge the secret. Willy's life might have been different as well. But Miller's play is not about hindsight. The irony is that Biff knows too much about his father who in turn knew too little about his own son.

Miller writes, "The assumption—or presumption—behind [my] plays is that life has meaning." (*Collected Plays* 8) Heading home alone from the restaurant, Willy makes meaning by choosing between two ideals which he cannot make compatible: he gives away his money and goes in search of seeds. "Nothing is planted," he tells Stanley, who at this moment is standing in for anyone paying attention, "I don't have a thing in the ground." Father and sons come home— separately—and conclude their aborted conversation begun in the restaurant. For Willy and Biff it is the final occasion to end the sound and fury between them and redeem the meaning of their relationship. Biff finds Willy in the garden in a scene that reminds critic Ronald Hayman of Shakespeare:

> One scene which demands powerful language is the late-night seed-planting scene.... Finally aware that he has ignored too long the call of the open air, Willy pathetically tries to plant seeds by torchlight. Had the dialogue been weakly written, this scene would merely have made him look ludicrous. Instead, madly talking to his dead brother, he is almost like a salesman-Lear on a garden/heath. The poetry spreads from the action to the language, which is simple, unpretentious, innocent of any rhetorical inflation, but pregnant, specific, and thoroughly effective. (Hayman 36)

Some readers are inclined to dismiss Willy's ravings in his "garden" as psychotic, but Miller insists that we must not.

Lamenting the "decision to play Willy as a psycho" in the Stanley Kramer film version of the play, Miller wrote:

> As a psychotic, he was predictable in the extreme; more than that, the misconception melted the tension between a man and his society.... If he was nuts, he could hardly stand as a comment on anything. (*Timebends* 315)

As Willy goes about measuring seed rows, he tells the ghost of Ben: "A man can't go out the way he came in, Ben, a man has got to add up to something." This is not a psychotic statement. Miller cited in his vision of the play "the image of a need greater than hunger or thirst, a need to leave a thumbprint somewhere on the world ... [even knowing that in doing so] one has carefully inscribed one's name on a cake of ice on a hot July day." (*Collected Plays* 29) In Willy's pain-wracked thinking he is planting (leaving a literal thumbprint on the earth) metaphorical seeds because his favored son has—under values he's symbolically abandoned in the restaurant—come to nothing.

Willy is planting a garden in an industrial landscape. It is obvious to link him here with Adam in—or being banished from—the first garden. Also easy to reject as a sentimental pastoral illusion is any notion of going back to a simpler life, of recovering the frontier, of making once again a connection to the land a central experience and value. But Miller has dramatized here some of the real consequences of living in a mechanized society and, as he stated in *"Salesman" in Beijing* and elsewhere, knows something inestimable and essential has been lost. Willy wants to open windows that are already open. What would he do in a contemporary building with windows that cannot be opened? Many people are drawn to Willy because he protests the loss of a beloved way of life and will not give up hope. Although Willy's failings undermine his chance for happiness is it not possible to see in his final act of planting seeds a warning—along with all the sad crazy confusion—too late for him but not for his audience, that we have collectively made a profound error about the values we live by?

Somewhere in the garden Willy falls irrevocably into the plan to end his life. With the help of Ben's ghost, Willy ponders the question of suicide as a cowardly act but settles it with another question: "Does it take more guts to stand here the rest of my life ringing up zero?" In Ben's presence Willy imagines death as a kind of pioneering journey into the dark wilderness where his insurance money will turns into diamonds and both his and Biff's life are redeemed. Of course Willy's thinking is fraught with confusion: it is a spiritual redemption gained through making himself a commodity; insurance companies may not pay for suicidal death; Biff need Willy's honesty and unconditional love more than he needs his money; and, what happens to Linda? Miller raises these issues quite plainly but appears to care more about the final moment of confrontation between Willy and Biff in which both are transfigured.

Raymond Williams writes, "The persuasive atmosphere of the play ... is one of false consciousness—the conditioned attitudes in which Loman trains his sons—being broken into by real consciousness, in actual life and relationships." (Corrigan, ed. 7) Biff has come home to tell the truth and in doing so to make himself free. Willy needs confirmation that he isn't "[going] out the way he came in, [that he does in fact] add up to something." When Biff furiously yells, "We never told the truth for ten minutes in this house!" he has broken through the false consciousness that afflicts the family. And when Willy responds to Biff's self-acknowledgement—"Pop! I'm a dime a dozen and so are you!"—he is confirming that he is not "[going] out the way he came in." Roudané writes:

Willy Loman's real condition lies in his insecurity in the universe, his profound sense of being unfulfilled.... No question Willy exaggerates, cheats, and lies, charges which he is ill equipped to refute but well suited to deny. But when he screams to Biff, 'I am not a dime a dozen! I am Willy Loman, and you are Biff Loman!" ... is he not laying claim, not only to his dignity and individual worth but also To every person's worthiness? (Bigsby, ed. 79)

This is not a perfect moment. Happy immediately tries to undo Biff's statement by insisting the family never lies—which is a lie in itself. And in the Requiem Happy shows no sign of change or insight. He vows to continue in his father's career path, perhaps more aggressively, as if to show "them" who the Loman men really are. But Biff will not follow in Willy's path. What Biff *will* do is unclear. He asks Willy to "let [him] go," and in the broken down rush of tears that comes as he holds on to Willy, the kind of love that permits this release finally flows between them. Miller called Willy's recognition of Biff's love an "epiphany." Describing a late rehearsal in China, Miller observes that his Willy-actor:

> has ceased to feel he is empty in the final confrontation scene with Biff, for the same reason none of us feels empty when love is in us. Willy is a lover forsaken and seeking a lost state of grace, and the great lift of the play is his discovery, in the unlikeliest moments of threats and conflict, that he is loved by his boy, his heart of hearts. (*"Salesman" in Beijing* 247)

The Requiem
Each of those at the gravesite responds characteristically. Practical Charley, probably unable to bear too much emotion, worries about the darkening day. Happy, speaking with his father's bizarrely combative style, takes Willy's death as a personal affront and nearly assaults Biff for speaking the truth. Biff is indirectly revealing his true self when he speaks the truth about his father; he is solicitous of his mother and knows about dreams. Linda has spent so much time protecting Willy from himself that she seems not to have understood his dreams, and now she does not understand what has befallen her. She is grief-stricken to find herself "free and clear" without him. Nearly mute with sorrow, and probably remembering Willy's story about Dave Singleman's famous funeral, she asks, "Why didn't anybody come?" Her love for her husband is almost palpable. Self-effacing Bernard stays in the background.

Some new and unexpected events occur in the Requiem.

Charley, whose sentences are always plain—even (like Willy's) cliché-ridden—suddenly becomes lyrical. Speaking as Miller might or possibly stirred by Biff's insight and a need to intervene against Happy's aggressiveness, Charley likens a salesman's condition to that of a lonely wanderer, not unlike that of a pioneer—being "way out there in the blue." Earlier he had reminded Willy that the "... only thing you got in this world is what you can sell." Charley reminds us now that in the culture of selling "No man only needs a little salary." And any man would feel "kind of temporary about [himself]." Biff, too, is different. Released now, by the truth-telling encounter with his father, to accept himself, Biff can remember and speak about what was good in his past. Released also from the frozen moment in Willy's mind where he was imprisoned by his father's self-serving adoration. Biff has recovered his history and this must happen before he can recover his life.

These insights and developments are the stuff of tragedy, but not of the classical kind. Miller was not concerned about this distinction, but many critics were and are. Their conflicting views and reflections are found abundantly in the extensive commentary generated by Miller's work. A range of opinion exists about Willy Loman. To Mary McCarthy, Willy is a "cut-out figure ..." typical of those inhabiting the American advertiser's view of American life. (McCarthy xv) Robert Hogan calls Willy a character of "rare meaningfulness." (Hogan 20) Benjamin Nelson writes:

Willy Loman is intrinsically American, but in his particularity he also attains universality. Shot through with weaknesses and faults, he is almost a personification of self-delusion and waste, the apotheosis of the modern man in an age too vast, demanding and complex for him. But without abrogating his intense individuality, he is also the archetypal father, not far removed in his hopes, mistakes, catastrophe, and reconciliation from that most ludicrous and sublime of all archetypal parents, King Lear. Finally, he personifies the human being's desire, for all his flaws, to force apart the steel pincers of necessity and partake of magnificence, and in this need he becomes a profoundly relevant man for all ages. (Nelson 134)

Willy has had a powerful effect on many audiences; people respond to him as if he were a real person. Miller tells a story about a famous retail magnate who was so affected by the play that at its conclusion he walked up to the front of the theatre to publicly announce that no employee in his firm would ever be fired because of his age. (*Timebends* 191) Miller also recalls the feelings he had while writing the play in some little outbuilding on his Connecticut homestead: "Stepping out the door exhausted at the end of a day [I looked] up at the night sky and said 'Talk to me, Willy, what should I say?' He seemed to be there in the woods, watching me through the leaves, standing there in his pleated trousers, felt hat, with the valises in the weeds." (*"Salesman" in Beijing* 251)

Works Cited

Bigsby, Christopher, ed. *Arthur Miller and Company*, London: Methuen Drama in association with the Arthur Miller Centre for American Studies, 1990.

———, ed. *Cambridge Companion to Arthur Miller*. New York: Cambridge University Press, 1997.

Brater, Enoch, "Miller's Realism and Death of a Salesman." *AM (20th Century Views): New Perspectives*. Ed. Robert A. Martin. Englewood Cliffs: Prentice Hall, 1982.

Carson, Neil. *Arthur Miller*. New York: St. Martin's Press, 1988.

Corrigan, Robert W., ed. *Arthur Miller: A Collection of Critical Essays*. Englewood Cliffs: Prentice Hall, 1969.

Driver, Tom. "Strengths and Weaknesses in Arthur Miller," *Tulane Drama Review* 4, no. 4, May, 1960.

Gantz, Arthur. *Realms of the Self: Variations on a Theme in Modern Drama*. New York: New York University Press, 1980.

Hansberry, Lorraine. "An Author's Reflections: Willy Loman, Walter Younger, and He Who Must Live," *Village Voice*, August 12, 1959, p. 7.

Hayman, Ronald. *Contemporary Playwrights: Arthur Miller*. London: Heineman Educational, 1970.

Hogan, Robert. *Arthur Miller*. Minneapolis: University of Minnesota Press, 1964.

McCarthy, Mary. *Sights and Spectacles*. New York: Farrar, Straus and Cudahy, 1956.

Miller, Arthur. *Collected Plays*. New York: Viking Press, 1981.

———. *"Salesman" in Beijing*. New York: Viking Press, 1984.

———. *Timebends*. New York: Grove Press, 1987.

Nelson, Benjamin. *Arthur Miller: Portrait of a Playwright*. London: Owen, 1970.

Porter, Thomas E. *Myth and Modern American Drama*. Detroit: Wayne State University Press, 1969.

Roudané, Matthew C, ed. *Approaches to Teaching Arthur Miller's "Death of a Salesman."* New York: Modern Language Association of America, 1995.

Rowe, Kenneth Thorpe. *A Theatre in Your Head*. New York: Funk & Wagnalls, 1964.

Critical Views

MARY MCCARTHY ON WILLY AS A "CAPITALIZED HUMAN BEING"

The typical character of the so-called American realist school belongs to the urban lower middle class sociologically, but biologically he is a member of some indeterminate lower order of primates. This creature is housed in a living-room filled with installment-plan furniture, some of which will be broken before the play is over. The sound of breakage and the sound of heavy breathing will signify "theatre." As directed by Elia Kazan, the whip-cracking ringmaster of this school of brutes, the hero is found standing with clenched fists, stage left, yelling at some member of his family, stage right, until one of them breaks into hysterical weeping and collapses onto a chair by the stage-center table, his great head buried in his hands. The weeping character is confessing to being alcoholic, homosexual, a failure.

Nobody anywhere has ever behaved like these people. This fact, somehow, is supposed to make them more "typical." A disturbing aspect of *Death of a Salesman* was that Willy Loman seemed to be Jewish, to judge by his speech-cadences, but there was no mention of this on the stage. He could not be Jewish because he had to be "America." All the living-rooms, backyards, stoops, and fire-escapes of the American School claim to be "America," while containing no particular, individualized persons of the kind that are found in the plays of other nations and in novels. The absence of any specific information seems to guarantee profundity. Most of these plays are sadistic fantasies in realistic disguise.

That is what makes their popularity so puzzling. The public seems to be, literally, a glutton for punishment.

A joke used to be told about a man in the theatre lobby after *Death of a Salesman* confiding to his companion: "That damned New England territory never was any good." This man elicits my sympathy because he was turning over in his mind the single solid fact divulged by the playwright: that Willy Loman sold something in the New England area.

Still, *Death of a Salesman* is the only play of the new American School that can be said to touch home. What is the matter with Willy Loman? Why is he so unhappy? "America" is what is wrong with him, Arthur Miller would answer, and to some extent this is true. The conception of the salesman's installment-plan home as a house of shabby lies and competitive boasts, growing hollower and hollower as old age and penury hem it in, is close to our national life; it is in fact precisely a close-up of the "home" depicted in full color by advertisers in the national magazines, with Father, Mother, two fine Kids, and the Product. But the play is wholly conceptualized, like the ads to which it gives a bitter retort. Parents, children, and neighbors are cut-out figures, types, equally in both versions of the American dream. Ideally, according to this formula, the play would be a kind of grim satire, the negative of the positive, keeping the same terms. *This is the way your pretty picture looks from the inside*, the playwright would be saying to the advertising men. Insofar as the play does this, it is arresting and moving in a sardonic way. The trouble is that it strives to be tragedy and becomes instead confused and hortatory.

"Attention must be paid," intones the shrill, singsong voice of the mother, ordering her sons to take notice of their father's plight. "Attention, attention, must finally be paid to such a person." She is really admonishing the audience that Willy is, as she says, "a human being." But that is just it; he is a capitalized Human Being without being anyone, a suffering animal who commands a helpless pity. The mother's voice raised in the age-old Jewish rhythms ("Attention must be paid," is not a normal English locution, nor is "finally" as it is used, nor is "such a person") seems to have drifted in from some other play that was about particular people. But Willy is only a type, demanding a statistical attention and generalized, impersonal condolence, like that of the editorial page. No one could write an editorial calling attention to the case of King

Lear. Yet the problem is the same: an old man, failing powers, thankless children, and a grandiose dream of being "well liked"—i.e., of being shown the proofs of love—that ends in utter isolation, ignominy, and madness. Lear, however, has the gift of language, the human, individual accent that is not a class endowment, for his Fool has it too. Lear is not any king; he is Lear. Willy Loman in the stage direction is called the Salesman. Which is more universal?

TOM DRIVER ON MILLER'S FAILURE TO EXPLORE THE ROOTS OF WILLY'S DOWNFALL

Miller lacks that inquisitiveness which would take him to the bottom of the problems he encounters. One might say that he sees the issues too soon, sees them in their preliminary form of social or even moral debate, but not in terms of dramatic events that disturb the audience's idea of basic truth, which is the foundation for its moral attitudes. It is the genius of a Pirandello, a Brecht, or an Ionesco to cause such disturbance and by doing so to become genuine moral critics. Miller's limited theatre fits down inside the theatre of the world which the audience inhabits. His theatre is too small to touch the outer walls against which the genuinely objective drama would need to be played.

This point is made very clear in certain remarks he makes about *Death of a Salesman*, especially as we compare them with the confusion which lurks in every corner of that play. The following passage occurs in a discussion of Willy Loman's stature as a tragic figure:

> How can we respect a man who goes to such extremities over something he could in no way help or prevent? The answer, I think, is not that we respect the man, but that we respect the Law he has so completely broken, wittingly or not, for it is that Law which, we believe, defines us as men. The confusion of some critics viewing *Death of a Salesman* in this regard is that they do

not see that Willy Loman has broken a law without whose protection life is insupportable if not incomprehensible to him and to many others; it is the law which says that a failure in society and in business has no right to live. Unlike the law against incest, the law of success is not administered by statute or church, but it is very nearly as powerful in its grip upon men. The confusion increases because, while it is a law, it is by no means a wholly agreeable one even as it is slavishly obeyed, for to fail is no longer to belong to society, in his estimate.

The confusion, I am afraid, lies not with the critics but with the playwright, and it is a very illustrative one. There is, in fact, no "law which says that a failure in society and in business has no right to live." It would, indeed, suit Miller's polemic better if there were. There is a *delusion* that a failure in society and in business has no right to live. To some people, such as Willy Loman, it may indeed seem like a law. But it is one thing for a character in a play to act as if something were a law, and quite another thing for the playwright to believe it. Miller's subsequent remarks in this same section of his essay make it perfectly clear that he himself, the audience, and also Willy Loman, do as a matter of fact have criteria according to which they suspect that this "law" is a hoax. It is in fact not a law but a false *credo*, which Willy shares with many persons, and the result of the attempt to make a false *credo* into a law results only in pathetic irony.

What is it, one wonders, that prevents Miller from probing Willy's consciousness and ours to the point of finding the truly objective world in which we still, in fact, believe and according to which Willy's "law" strikes us as so pathetic? If we ask where in the play one touches bedrock, the answer is nowhere. Is the law of success *really* a law? No. Miller tells us that "the system of love," which is "embodied in Biff Loman" was meant to counter Willy's "law." But if that is true, it was unfortunately not dramatized. That is, the way in which Biff's "law" of love judges and invalidates Willy's "law" of success is not revealed, and so the one is not actually a truth which is being brought to bear dramatically on the other.

The same ambiguity is seen in the question of society versus the individual. John Gassner said long ago that Arthur Miller had "split his play between *social causation* and *individual responsibility* for Willy's fate."[1] Is Willy's "law" the result of some defect in himself? If so, what is the nature of this defect, and what genuine law does it confound? Or is his "law" imposed upon him by a white-collar industrial society? If so, what is wrong with such a society and what truth does it prevent Willy Loman from seeing? Miller would probably resist making a decision in favor of either the individual or the social causation, and rightly so. But in that case, if he is interested in theatre worth the name of art, he has an obligation to examine his complex situation until the roots of Willy's anxiety are exposed, an exposure which would cause us to know something about the reality in which we are, if only unconsciously, living. It is in the lack of penetration into the objective philosophical situation that Miller fails us, with the result that we must settle for no more enlightenment upon our situation than pathetic Willy had upon his.

Note
1. *The Theatre in Our Times*, New York, 1954, p. 347. Author's italics.

DENNIS WELLAND ON THE WEAK EVIDENCE FOR A MARXIST INTERPRETATION

The evidence for a Marxist interpretation of *Death of a Salesman* is, in any case, not very impressive. The scene in which Willy, seeking a change of job, is unceremoniously dismissed can hardly have been intended as the indictment of capitalism that Miss Clark thinks it. Theatrically it is a moving, even painful, scene, but it engenders a mixture of pity and exasperation rather than the indignation that we would expect of "party-line literature." Willy's behaviour is not calculated to enhance his or our sense of his personal dignity: even as we pity him for his despairing reduction of the wage he will settle for, we are exasperated by his inability to see that he is throwing away any chance he may have by his obtuse mishandling of Howard. The central irony of this scene resides in the discrepancy between Howard and our preconceived idea of the capitalist tycoon. This is no ruthless executive callously firing the trusted employee from calculated mercenary motives: it is the "nice guy" forced into a situation that he doesn't know how to handle "nicely" and consequently only making the ugliness of it worse. It is one little man being fired by another little man, Willy being fired by a younger Willy. Howard's callousness is occasioned less by his business acumen than by his absorption in his personal life. The tape-recorder serves two purposes in the scene: when Willy stumbles against it and sets it accidentally into motion it precipitates an hysterical breakdown that symbolises the central theme of the play in Willy's horror at his inability to switch it off—to switch off the recorded past. Whether the past is that of his own sons recorded on his memory and conscience, or that of Howard's son recorded on a mechanical instrument, it is the past, more than capitalism, of which Willy is always the victim. The machine also provides a means of dramatising Howard's ingenuous pride in his children. They are far more real to him than is the memory of his father to which Willy constantly appeals, and his pride in their prowess and their affection for him obliterates any understanding of Willy's plight, exactly as Willy's pride in his sons has blinded him to any recognition of the worth of Bernard. This point is emphasised by Howard's automatic question, "Why don't your sons give you a hand?" and by the immediate introduction of the Ben-*motif* as a further reproach to Willy's vacillatory sentimentality. Moreover, this memory-sequence dissolves into the actuality of Charley's office, where a successful Bernard on his way to professional and social triumphs in Washington unintentionally prompts Willy into another orgy of envious recrimination at everybody except him. The irony set in motion in Howard's office culminates in Charley's, for it is Charley, not Howard, who is the nearest thing to the big business-man in this play, and yet Charley is the only person who offers Willy any positive help. The money he advances him and the employment he offers have no strings attached: Willy's acceptance of the one and rejection of the other is the outcome of a very curious sense of personal dignity, but there is no mistaking the truth of his exit line:

> WILLY [*on the verge of tears*]: Charley, you're the only friend I got. Isn't that a remarkable thing?[4]

It is remarkable to Willy not only because he has never had any time for Charley, but because Charley is the exact antithesis of himself. To describe Charley as the Horatio to Willy's Hamlet (as one critic at least has done) is to put it too romantically, but the antithesis is clearly and succinctly drawn by Willy's exchange with Charley over Bernard's success:

> WILLY: And you never told him what to do, did you? You never took any interest in him.
> CHARLEY: My salvation is that I never took any interest in anything. There's some money—fifty dollars. I got an accountant inside.[5]

Charley the successful business-man is the only person who understands Willy the failed salesman, but he understands him in a wholly unsentimental way quite different from the "interest" that is Willy's more characteristic response. He will help Willy with a job or with money, but he will not tell him what to do: he expects Willy, like Bernard, to make his own choice. Having subordinated sentiment to business efficiency all his life, Charley can allow his feelings to come through at Willy's funeral, and his final speech, "Nobody dast blame this man ...," though it is not the moral of the play, ought to have made unnecessary Miller's prefatory disavowal of any intended arraignment of big business.[6]

Notes

4. *C.P.*, p. 193.

5. *C.P.*, p. 191.

6. *C.P.*, pp. 221, 31, 37.

ERIC MOTTRAM ON AMBIGUITY IN MILLER'S PRESENTATION OF TRAGEDY VERSUS SOCIAL REFORM

Miller once remarked: "I can't live apart from the world." Yet his plays dramatize the ways in which a man alienates himself from his society and fights to get back into it. Until his most recent play, the structure of that society goes uncondemned and unanalysed, taken as if it were an unchangeable artefact. The weight of action falls cruelly on the individual within the fixed, powerful society which fails to support him at his moment of need and remains, as he falls, monolithically immovable. "Evil" is those social pressures which conflict with an equally vaguely defined individual integrity in the hero or heroine. But critical though he is of American, perhaps Western, values, Miller finally has come to believe that "evil" is really the natural cruelty of human nature seen, not as a product of historical social structures, but as inevitable data. (...)

[In *Death of a Salesman*] once again Miller leaves the conflict between a man and his society hanging fire between suicide and an intolerably unchanging world. He scores his points, with undoubted success, through a system of language which repeats ordinary catch-phrases and shared jargon, manipulated to cover the facts. (...)

Death of a Salesman uses flashbacks within an expressionist set in order to present the contents of the sixty-year-old hero's mind as he draws towards suicide after self-perceived wasted life. Again, the waste is not countered with any suggestion of radical change in the society's ethic which caused it. We are offered only the wife's cry of warning to her two sons in Act I:

> I don't say he's a great man. Willy Loman never made a lot of money. His name was never in the paper. He's not the finest character that ever lived. But he's a human being, and a terrible thing is happening to him. So attention must be paid. He's not to be allowed to fall into his grave like an old dog. Attention, attention must finally be paid to such a person. You called him crazy ... a lot of people think he's lost his balance. But you don't have to be very smart to know what his trouble is. The man is exhausted ... A small man can be just as exhausted as a great man. (pp. 162–63)

But what terrible thing has happened to Loman, what attention must be paid, what has exhausted him, and what kind of balance has he lost? He is not a murderer like Keller, but he too reaches the shocking realization that his life has been work and for nothing. Loman has been unable to learn that business ethics, the morality of his work-community, oppose the traditions he assumed were still in action: the personal ethic of honour, the patriarchal nature of a basically benevolent society and family, and neighbourhood relations. He speaks the very language of that acquisitive society, without hypocrisy, the terminology of the world which throws him off-balance.

Miller presents a fairly full context for the suicide, but he cannot show his hero attaining any profound understanding of his end. Loman's father made flutes and sold them himself throughout the States in the self-made businessman's manner. Loman's brother Ben is the next stage: the man self-made outside America: "Why, boys, when I was seventeen I walked into the jungle, and when I was twenty-one I walked out. [*He laughs.*] And by God I was rich" (p. 157). In stage three, the jungle is New York, the American city, where a man stays, burdened by a house overtopped by skyscrapers, household payments on equipment with built-in obsolescence, mortgage and insurance worries, and a built-in belief that the competitive society is life itself at its best. As in *All My Sons*, the son penetrates some of the father's illusions. Biff Loman tried life on a Texas ranch but remained inhibited by his father's standards. In a flashback Miller presents the father–son relationship as a manic cult of youthful athletic prowess operated at the expense of maturity, with Dad as the great pal and Mother the source of binding love. Miller's criticism, as far as it goes, emerges from the conflict between youth and age, private and public life, optimism and suicidal despair. Like Keller, Loman perceives he has "accomplished" nothing, but it is still "the greatest country in the world" even if "personal attractiveness" gets you nowhere. He perceives that "the competition is maddening," but he refers here to the uncontrolled birthrate only. His second son, Happy, is also a salesman, already lost to booze and sex, obsessed with the empty word "future," always on his lips.

But the boys are only in their thirties, and at least Biff knows he is still "like a boy," as his father is, locked in the national myth of youthfulness. Once a Loman's energy is drained by his society he is thrown aside, in this case casually sacked by the son of the man who has been his boss for thirty-four years. He protests: "You can't eat the orange and throw the peel away—a man is not a piece of fruit!" He is wrong, but Miller cannot find anyone to help him. The language itself blocks understanding: "well-liked," "create personal interest," making "an appearance," "knocking 'em cold." The appalling hypnotic power of such repeated terms is the action of a deadly stifling of vitality in the name of optimism. Loman's exhaustion is the tiredness of empty buoyancy, of feeling "kind of temporary" about himself. His wife provides loving despair; Biff knows he is a "fake."

Lost honour and comradeship permeate Miller's work. His men live on a vision they cannot make work. Loman lives in a world where his sons are Adonises, with Biff on the football field in a golden helmet "like a young god—something like that. And the sun, the sun all around him." But the boys' old school friend Bernard, who worked at his books, is now defending a case in the Supreme Court, and it is Charley, his father and Loman's old friend, who says outright that personal relations and codes of honour are meaningless now:

> Why must everybody like you? Who liked J. P. Morgan? Was he impressive? In a Turkish bath he'd look like a butcher. But with his pockets on he was very well liked. (p. 192)

But Loman is beyond advice and change; in fact he is dead already, believing that, through his insurance, he is worth more, in cash, dead than alive, and this at least would atone for his cruelty to his wife and betrayal of his sons. It now comes out that Biff lost the will to live when he saw his father with a tart, and lost the will to pass his exams: "we never told the truth for ten minutes in this house" (p. 216). They are all victims of a "phoney dream" and it is the American dream.

Happy still believes his father was right, even after the suicide, and many of Miller's audience must have agreed in their hearts. But Loman is what happens to an ordinarily uneducated man in an unjust competitive society in which men are victimized by false gods. His fate is not tragic. There is nothing of the superhuman or providential or destined in this play. Everyone fails in a waste of misplaced energy. A travelling salesman is on record with a good criticism of the play: "that damned New England territory never was any good." But other men made another criticism (in the phone calls, letters and telegrams Miller received): "I saw your play. I've just quit my job. What do I do now?" One man said, "Why didn't Willy Loman go to the Household Finance Corporation and solve all his problems?" Two large corporations asked Miller to address their sales meetings. Earlier, *All My Sons* had been picketed by the Catholic Veterans and the American Legion. Times change. But Miller's message is ambiguous: Loman may be "uneducated" and the victim of a "vulgar idea of success," but the system which fails him is "inevitable," as inevitable as the world of Dreiser's Clyde Griffith.

Miller presents *Death of a Salesman* and *All My Sons* in a spirit of puzzled, anguished analysis but does not suggest to his

Broadway audience that anything so radical as revolutionary change in American terminal society might be necessary. In his essay, "Tragedy and the Common Man," contemporary with *Death of a Salesman*, he repudiates the idea that "the tragic mode is archaic" owing to the absence of socially elevated heroes and the advent of habits of scepticism and analysis. He vaguely refers to modern psychiatric uses of Oedipus and Orestes complexes which "apply to everyone in similar emotional situations." This acceptance of muddled notions of Greek tragedy and modern psychology leads him to plump for that old stand-by for the American liberal, "the individual," once again comfortably unexamined:

> I think tragic feeling is evoked in us when we are in the presence of a character who is ready to lay down his life, if need be, to secure one thing—his sense of personal dignity. From Orestes to Hamlet, Medea to Macbeth, the underlying struggle is that of the individual attempting to gain his "rightful" position in his society.

But if the hero dies at his own hand, with the sense of waste and bewilderment still entire within him, who can now be interested in anything but the chance of changing the values of the society that brings him to that degradation? The hero's challenge today threatens the hierarchical determinations of the controllers of society and their representatives, the play's backers and audiences.

> Tragedy is the consequence of a man's total compulsion to evaluate himself justly.

But if that evaluation must take place in a structure of injustice, of subservience as a wage-slave, of self-help within an economic structure which limits or denies the hero's self-fulfilment, and of an ideology which determines only that some men are more equal than others, then you have the dilemma of Miller's plays: not tragedies but plays of partial awakening to fate before a conclusion in suicidal waste. Miller believes that the tragic flaw (itself a misreading of classical theory) is not weakness but "inherent unwillingness to remain passive." The passive, therefore, are flawless and the majority are passive; Miller realizes accurately that the "terror" of this kind of life lies in "the total onslaught by an individual against the seemingly stable cosmos surrounding us ... the 'unchangeable' environment." But surely the "evil" lies in those who perpetuate this environment, passively or actively. If the plot is not to be simply a mocking of the non-passive man, it must show a real chance of heroism and change. This Miller fails to do. "The thrust for freedom," he says, "is the quality in tragedy which exalts. The revolutionary questioning of the stable environment is what terrifies. In no way is the common man debarred from such thoughts or such action." But the common man is liable to arouse only pity as a poor fool in terror for his life unless he is allowed an understanding that his revolt is towards ends which have a specific chance of attainment. Otherwise the context is rigid sterility.

At least Miller does not degrade human life in the manner of Broadway psycho-drama which claims that self-analysis cures everything, or of the social melodrama which claims that economic change predicates total human change. He wants theatre to present "a balanced concept of life" in which the hero's need is "to wholly realize himself" without the questioning author preaching revolution. Consequently, when Loman is betrayed by the myths and ethic of his society, all we are given is his wife's pitiful cry: "Attention, attention must finally be paid to such a person."

BENJAMIN NELSON ON MILLER'S USE OF DRAMATIC FORM

The structure is a blend of naturalism and expressionism, resulting in an extremely powerful and highly personal form. Although rooted in realistic convention, the play extends the borders of realism without straining credibility because it is mirroring the processes of a disoriented mind. Thus, the form of *Death of a Salesman* is perfectly suited to the nature of its protagonist's psychological imbalance, in which the memory of the past challenges the reality of the present in a surrealistic battle for supremacy.

One important manifestation of this structure is the breakdown of chronological time in order to dredge the important elements from the past into the troubled present. This is not a simple flashback technique by which Willy's life is presented in a neat linear development but rather a complex interrelationship of past and present, illusion and reality, through which character and event emerge concentrically, almost kaleidoscopically, out of the vast whirlpool of Willy's semiconscious existence.

This form is integral to the theme and characterization of the play in at least two ways. First, it indicates the agonizing intensity of the salesman's search for the meaning of his life. He recreates incidents and individuals as if they were all witnesses at an inquest, and reaches out to them in an almost delirious attempt to find answers for his fall.

The second important consequence of *Death of a Salesman*'s structure is that by insolubly linking the final days of Willy's life with the years that have shaped them, it gives his life and death a dramatic cohesiveness. Classically, Miller introduces his protagonist shortly before his destruction, but by *showing* the audience Willy's life instead of piecing it together through exposition, the playwright escapes the snare of wordiness and the long, ponderous development which was necessary to the meaning but detrimental to the effectiveness of *All My Sons*. The suspense that would ordinarily precede Willy's death is eradicated, but as the play's title indicates, Miller did not intend the ending to come as a surprise. More pertinently, the salesman's suicide is graphically joined to the past events which have paved its way.

Miller does not ask the audience to make an unqualified emotional identification with his beleaguered hero. Although the play's power lies in its stunning ability to elicit this sympathy, the intensely idiosyncratic portrait of Willy Loman is a constant reminder that the meaning of his drama depends upon our clear awareness of the limitations of Willy's life and vision. The flashbacks are not scattered through the play at random. Even though Miller does not present them in any tidy chronological order, he selects and arranges them in a definite pattern that gives increasing depth and dimension to the protagonist while simultaneously illuminating the contradictions in his character which continually evade Willy's subjective scrutiny. Emerging out of 1928, the watershed year of Willy's life, each flashback sequence moves us deeper into Willy's consciousness and leads finally to the scene involving Biff's discovery of his adultery, the episode that would understandably issue last out of Willy's recollections since it is the one memory he has tried hardest to repress.

Essentially the flashbacks fall into two categories, each defining a crucial facet of Willy's life. One grouping comprises the events involving Willy and his brother Ben, who appears to Willy's crumbling mind as a cold, righteous, self-assured deity, an objectification by contrast of Willy's uncertainty and insecurity. In every confrontation with Ben, Willy is portrayed as the adoring, fearful, and supplicating child seeking guidance and assurance from the archetypal authoritarian father. Guidance is also the keynote of the second set of flashbacks, but in these Willy is dispensing advice rather than seeking it. This series of episodes, which centers on Willy and his sons, shows Willy the father trying to substantiate his ecstatic belief in the success ideal by superimposing it upon his children.

Both sets of flashbacks culminate in the one involving Willy's infidelity—the fact and symbol of his final degradation, the revelation of his insecurity and failure, and the verification of his bleak loneliness and alienation. Ultimately each event dredged out of his past makes the same point about Willy Loman: his life is caught in an unresolvable dichotomy between fact and fancy. He is unable to separate his individuality from his conception of himself as a supersalesman because he cannot truly differentiate between the two.

Willy's life is a patchwork of errors in judgment, mental and moral lapses, and misdirected hopes, but perhaps his greatest mistake is living far too long with the wrong dream.

Miller's characters delineate personal qualities through their particular usage of commonplace words and idioms: their language style reflects their style of conduct. Applications of this principle in *Death of a Salesman* range from the elementary to the sophisticated. At the elementary level there are a few explicit evaluations of the protagonist. Linda, for example, recites this estimate: "I don't say he's a great man. Willy Loman never made a lot of money. His name was never in the paper. He's not the finest character that ever lived. But he's a human being, and a terrible thing is happening to him.... A small man can be just as exhausted as a great man." ("He's only a little boat looking for a harbor," she adds later.) Charley also generalizes in plain terms: "Willy was a salesman. And for a salesman, there is no rock bottom to the life. He don't put a bolt to a nut, he don't tell you the law or give you medicine. He's a man way out there in the blue, riding on a smile and a shoeshine." Whatever the accuracy of such evaluations, the trite metaphors and informal syntax, at least, are appropriate to the subject.

The speech of almost everyone in the play mirrors a class, a generation, and a way of life. "The boss is goin' crazy what kinda leak he's got in the cash register," a waiter relates; "you put it in but it don't come out." Clichés are abundant. Hap Loman is "gonna beat this racket" and come out "number-one man" in order to prove that his father "did not die in vain." His father excels in his command of tasteless cant popular in the 1930s. "Well, bottoms up! ... And keep your pores open!" Willy calls, saluting his lady friend. His most sorrowful laments are stock phrases: "where are you guys, where are you?" he shouts to his sons; "the woods are burning!" When he gropes for metaphoric originality, he cannot escape staleness: "because you got a greatness in you, Biff, remember that.... Like a young God. Hercules—something like that. And the sun, the sun all around him." All the Lomans try to be eloquent by leavening their lower-middle-class Brooklyn dialect with high-class diction. They find words like "vengeful," "solidified," "consumes," "reconstruct," and "prohibit" (Willy), "feasible" and "characteristic" (Hap), "remiss" and "abrupt" (Biff), "crestfallen" and "conquer" (Linda). In context, unhappily for the speaker, such terms often sound incongruous.

Judged by these mannerisms, which Miller undoubtedly heard in his own social milieu, Willy Loman can be seen simply as a mediocrity native to American society. But Miller's objective, as in *All My Sons*, goes beyond linguistic realism. The author customarily underscores his characters' banality with hackneyed phrases and platitudes; here he practices that form of irony so deftly that even the vaguest generalization becomes an instrument for self-exposition.

Willy makes the superficiality of his belief in "personal attractiveness" clear through the way he advertises it. Childlike, he gains assurance by repeating facile success formulas: "it's not what you do, Ben. It's who you know and the smile on your face! It's contacts, Ben, contacts! ... A man can end with diamonds here on the basis of being liked!" His trite slogans claim the rhythm as well as the wisdom of aphorisms. "Because the man who makes an appearance in the business world," he hopefully pontificates, "the man who creates personal interest, is the man who gets ahead. Be liked and you will never want." He invokes supposedly potent words as if repeating them would bring into existence the desired actualities: "I realized that selling was the greatest career a man could want.... There was personality in it, Howard. There was respect, and comradeship, and gratitude in it." Even his sons' names betoken his hearty, naïve optimism. His wife and younger son, indeed, echo the favorite magical cliché; Happy's compliment to Biff and Linda's to Willy is "you're well liked."

If the Lomans' favorite adjective is "well liked," one of their commonest—and most revealing—verbs is "make." This verb occurs forty-five times in thirty-three different usages ranging from standard English to slang-expressions such as "make mountains out of molehills," "makin' a hit," "makin' my future," "make me laugh," and "make a train." In the play this wide range of meanings tends to accent a materialistic business ethic. The various denotations are reducible to four general categories—fabrication, causation, execution, and acquisition. Since "a salesman," in Charley's words, "don't put a bolt to a nut, ... tell you the law or give you medicine," Willy's attitude toward professional achievement stresses acquisition. "Make money" occurs no less than nine times, in addition to instances of seven related idioms like "make a living," "make good," "make the grade," "make a mark," and (simply) "make it." In context, furthermore, a majority of the usages denoting the other three primary senses *imply* attainment (or nonattainment) of success and money as, in the sense of execution, "the man who makes an appearance," "make a nice impression," and "you didn't make me, Willy. I picked you." Self-respect often depends, in Miller's works, upon constructive labor; here twenty-three idiomatic variants of a single verb (thirty-four examples in all) reiterate a contrary interpretation.

Arthur Miller on Producing *Death of a Salesman* in China

Why was *Salesman* chosen? Was it as propaganda against the American way of life? Is it really possible for Chinese to relate to the very American situation and to Willy Loman's character? Do Chinese actors work differently from Americans in creating their roles? Is the humor likely to register? Are there really any parallels in Chinese society? (...)

I theorize a universality of human emotions; I hope that the production here of this very American play will simply assert the idea of a single humanity once again.

At this point I can only say that the actors seem to have no difficulty in putting themselves into the parts; there must surely be some exotic mysteries for them in this play, but, after all, the Chinese practically invented the family, which is the core of the play, and the social interrelationships with the family struggle have been a part of Chinese life for a very long time.

As for the humor, at least the cast is laughing when laughter is called for, so I presume we have a chance to do the same with an audience. Parallels exist in the play with Chinese society, I have reason to think, assuming that people want to rise in the world everywhere. And if there aren't as yet traveling salesmen in this country, I conjecture that the idea of such a man is easily enough grasped from the text itself. In any case, the salesman motif is in some great part metaphorical; we must all sell ourselves, convince the world of a persona that perhaps we only wish we really possessed. (...)

I let myself say [to the actors] that the one red line connecting everyone in the play was a love for Willy; not admiration, necessarily, but a kind of visceral recognition that in his fumbling and often ridiculous way he is trying to lift up a belief in immense redeeming human possibilities. People can't stand him often, they flee from him, but they miss him when he isn't there. Perhaps it's that he hasn't a cynical bone in his body, he is the walking believer, the bearer of a flame whose going-out would leave us flat, with merely what the past has given us. He is forever signaling to a future that he cannot describe and will not live to see, but he is in love with it all the same.

Death of a Salesman, really, is a love story between a man and his son, and in a crazy way between both of them and America. (...)

Biff, after what for Chinese actors is a very short rehearsal period, says he has particularized, narrowed the area of mystery in his relation to Willy; it comes down to the question why he feels he has to return home at all when he knows how hard it will be to get along with the old man. What is Biff's need, what is the burden that only his father can help him unload? (As noted, I had been after all of them to begin breaking into their "generalized" behavior.)

I explain once again that this is a love story; that away from home he sometimes feels a painfully unrequited love for his father, a sense of something unfinished between them bringing feelings of guilt.

The actor says he understands this, that it is very Chinese.

"But why are you guilty, can you say?"

"Because I condemned Willy. I turned my father away," Ying translates.

"That's it. That's wonderful. What else?"

The actor shakes his head, says something to Ying Ruocheng, who tells me, "He doesn't know."

"It's like needing somebody's blessing before you can enjoy doing a certain thing. You want Willy to say, 'Yes, you should live in the West, you should not have to chase after the dollar, you should live your own life.' In other words, your love for him binds you; but you want it to free you to be your own man. But Willy would have to turn away from his own values, wouldn't he, to give you his blessing?"

He nods to me, says he understands this, and he seems excited by it, but I know there is something more to be said, something that will fill him with the anger he needs at the climaxes. I need something personal, intimate, something Chinese for him to grasp and use. The cast, as usual, is looking on and listening; it occurs to me that once again the Cultural Revolution might be an apt analogy. "It's like the dilemma of the Cultural Revolution; Jiang Qing's leadership was also full of self-deluded demands on you, wasn't it?" They all come alert as Ying translates. "She also claimed to be acting out of devotion to China, and that may have been what she felt, for all we know. Just like Willy, who believes he is trying to help you, not himself. But no matter how you tried to obey her and come up to the regime's expectations, you had to see that objectively China's economy was falling apart, her arts, commerce, the whole civilization going down the drain. And your father, Mao, seemed to be backing her, isn't that right? The point is, you felt a powerful frustration, didn't you, an anger that nobody was able to tear away that complex of half-truths and deceptions to raise up the truth before the people—before Mao himself!—the facts of the destruction going on. And maybe this is why Deng Xiaoping is using the slogan 'Truth from Facts,' rather than from ideology." A laughter of recognition up and down the row of chairs. "Biff is trying to do something very similar—tear Willy away from his ideology to face himself and you in detail, as a real individual who is at a certain time in his life. You can use the same Cultural Revolution frustration, that feeling of anger and the violence in you, in this role. The same thwarted love." (...)

What is turning out to ne universal—unless I am going to be brutally disappointed on opening night—is emotion rather than "facts." Linda, for example, is thoroughly on target now, no longer Willy's whimpering doormat. She has told me that she had the wrong idea of the woman to start with. Instead, she has become, as he calls her, "my foundation and support," who is fighting off his death from the outset, the only one who knows that he has attempted suicide and has connected a device to the gas heater that, should the mood overtake him completely, he might use. Linda's part has often been weakly played, as though she were a mere follower, but that is unlikely to happen when the actress keeps herself aware of what the script has told her she knows. The "fact" in this case is a completely exotic gas heater for water, something that these Chinese have never seen (and, indeed, has probably ceased to exist anymore in the States) but which they easily understand once I describe its design and operation. In any case, its strangeness does not for an instant interfere with our Chinese Linda's eventual understanding of the kind of woman she has to play—the kind who is strong by concealing her strength.

BRENDA MURPHY ON THE ORIGINAL PRODUCTION OF *DEATH OF A SALESMAN*

Miller has spoken often of the initial image of the play that was called at one early point in its development *The Inside of His Head*. The image "was of an enormous face the height of the proscenium arch which would appear and then open up, and we would see the inside of a man's head ... it was conceived half in laughter, for the inside of his head was a mass of contradictions."[4] The image is a clear visual representation of expressionism, the dramatization of subjective reality, in direct opposition to the realism in which Miller had composed *All My*

Sons. Miller did not want, however, to represent Willy's experience as a subjective nightmare, detached from the reality around him, which is the usual method of expressionism. Miller said in an interview that, while he had been moved by expressionist plays, he found the traditional expressionist aesthetic perverse: "there are no people in it any more ... it's the bitter end of the world where man is a voice of his class function, and that's it."[5]

In *Salesman*, Miller was after a more complex representation. He wanted the audience to see reality as Willy saw it, but also to recognize it as objectively real. Onstage there would be three epistemological levels: Willy's fantasies of the past, Willy's perception of the present, and the audience's perception of present stage-reality. Miller needed a dramatic form that would combine the subjectivity of expressionism with the illusion of objectivity afforded by realism.

One important step in the development of his form was going with director Elia Kazan to see Tennessee Williams's *A Streetcar Named Desire* during its New Haven preview in November of 1947. Miller has written that *Streetcar* "opened one specific door for me ... the words and their liberation, the joy of the writer in writing them, the radiant eloquence of its composition" (*T* 182). This new freedom in the use of language was clearly important to the poetry of the mundane that infuses Salesman, but Kazan has suggested an even more important contribution. After seeing the performance, he wrote, Miller "appeared to be full of wonder at the theatre's expressive possibilities. He told me he was amazed at how simply and successfully the non-realistic elements in the play—'*Flores! Flores para los muertos!*'—blended with the realistic ones."[6] *Streetcar*'s style of subjective realism, which Kazan and Williams had created with designer Jo Mielziner, went a long way toward solving Miller's dramatic and theatrical problems.

Subjective realism provides an anchor in reality—a series of events that are accepted by the audience as the objective reality of the play—but presents them through the mediating consciousness of a single character, a Blanche DuBois or a Willy Loman, whose mind is often in the process of breaking down. While the audience can share the nightmare experience of the protagonist, it never quite loses touch with the "real" events that the character is interpreting in what is perceived to be a distorted way. As Miller puts it, Willy "is literally at that terrible moment when the voice of the past is no longer distant but quite as loud as the voice of the present ... the form, therefore, is this process, instead of being a once-removed summation or indication of it" (*TE* 138). From this dual perspective, the audience can both empathize with the character's ordeal and judge it objectively. This mode of drama combines the strengths of expressionism with those of realism. Miller has explained, "*Death of a Salesman* was conceived literally on two dimensions at the same time. On one level there are autonomous characters while on another there are characters who exist as symbols for Willy Loman" (CB 59).

Notes

4. Arthur Miller, "Introduction," *Arthur Miller's Collected Plays* (New York: Viking, 1957), 135. Reprinted in Robert A. Martin, ed., *The Theater Essays of Arthur Miller* (New York: Viking, 1978), 267–68 (subsequently cited in the text as *TE*).

5. Olga Carlisle and Rose Styron, "Arthur Miller: An Interview," *Paris Review* 10 (Summer 1966). Reprinted in Martin, *The Theater Essays*, 135.

6. *Elia Kazan: A Life* (New York: Knopf, 1988), 361. Subsequently cited in the text as *K*.

MATTHEW ROUDANÉ ON THE EFFECTS OF STAGE SETTING AND DIRECTIONS

The set and the stage directions

Miller underpins the tragic power of the play through the wonderfully multivalent set and setting. When theatregoers settled into their seats at the packed Morosco Theatre on opening night in 1949 and waited for the play to begin, they heard the melody of a flute. The aural dissolves (like Willy's dreams) to the visual as the curtain rises and the salesman's skeletal house comes into focus. Elia Kazan and Miller worked meticulously with Jo Mielziner, who developed the set, and Eddie Kook, the lighting engineer. Miller provides one of the best-known opening stage directions in American drama, directions on which Kazan, Mielziner, and Kook based their collaborative efforts. Functioning as a kind of prose-poem, the initial stage directions prefigure many of the play's major dynamics.

The stage directions function in at least two important ways. First, they delineate the spatial and physical machinery of the play, including the basic layout of props, the importance of the forestage, the use of such kinesic devices as music and lighting, and, above all, the centrality of the salesman's house. Mielziner filled the stage with realistic props: a kitchen table with three chairs, a small refrigerator, telephone, wastebasket, stairs, three beds, an athletic trophy, and a chest of drawers. But these realistic props were placed within a highly expressionistic set. No solid walls separated Willy and Linda's bedroom, situated slightly elevated and stage right from the kitchen, or the boys' bedroom, located on the second floor, from the kitchen. Instead of a solid roof, only gabled rafters angling upwards, silhouetting a roof line, were used. The back of each room had walls of sorts, but they were translucent backdrops. Since no walls separated the rooms, characters were not necessarily confined spatially or, in the daydream sequences, temporally. When the action occurs in time present, for instance, the actors observe the imaginary wall-lines. But, Miller's stage directions indicate, "*in the scenes of the past these boundaries are broken, and characters enter or leave a room by stepping 'through' a wall onto the forestage*" (*Death of a Salesman*, p. 12).

Audiences gazed at another backdrop behind the house, which featured two trees and images of towering buildings. During Willy's daydreams about the past, Mielziner bathed the stage in a soft amber light, its golden hues suggesting the glory of a past in which the Lomans' neighborhood was filled with grass, trees with green leaves, and a beautiful horizon. The past was a time of freshly painted cars, homes, and soaring hopes. Biff proudly donned his golden football uniform before adoring fans. It was a time when Linda smiled easily. The idealism and happiness of the past have been leeched from the Lomans' present, however. Now, Linda enamels herself with her "*iron repression*" (p. 12). Often during the present scenes, lights from the rear cover the stage with an ominous reddish orange glow. These lighting gradations permit the spatial, the temporal, and the thematic to inhabit the stage simultaneously, and in ways that perfectly suggest the interiority of the characters. The shifts in lighting, if subtly done, not only make for a spatial fluidity, but also register through direct, sensory experience the cohering of social, psychic, and actual time.

A particularly foreboding scene illustrates Miller's dramaturgy. The menacing gas heater, located behind a translucent backdrop, visually seems to come alive at the end of Act One. The time is in the present as Biff enters that darkened kitchen, lights a cigarette, and walks downstage into "*a golden pool of light*" (p. 68). At the same time Willy and Linda are in their bedroom, reminiscing about the charisma Biff exuded in high school; Willy says that his son was

> Like a young god. Hercules—something like that. And the sun, the sun all around him. Remember how he waved to me? Right up from the field, with the representatives of three colleges standing by? And the buyers I brought, and the cheers when he came out—Loman, Loman, Loman! God Almighty, he'll be great yet. A star like that, magnificent, can never fade away! (p. 68)

When Willy utters the "never fade away" lines, however, Kook slowly dimmed the lights that were pointed at Willy, a haunting visual intimation that Linda is helping her husband to bed for the last time. Miller's stage direction accentuates the effect as the "gas heater begins to glow through the kitchen wall, near the stairs, a blue flame beneath red coils" (p. 68). Moments later a horrified Biff discovers the rubber tubing

Willy hides behind the gas heater. Visually, such stage atmosphere makes for brilliant theatrics. With props, lighting, body movement, and language operating contrapuntally, Miller draws the audience into the Lomans' holy storm.

The initial stage directions function in a second important way. They foreground, through metaphor, many of the play's deeper ambiguities and conflicts. The flute music sounds *"small and fine, telling of grass and trees and the horizon"* (p. 11). The music holds important past references for Willy: his father made and sold flutes as a traveling salesman; through a kind of free associative pattern, the music reveals something of Willy's past desires and dreams, when all things seemed possible to him. Once the music fades, the stage directions concentrate on the house itself, a "small, fragile-seeming home," a home dwarfed by the *"solid vault of apartment houses"* (p. 11). The vault allusion, whether referring ironically to a site of banking, investing, and finance, or to a site of entombment, entrapment, a place of no exit, clearly draws attention to the fragility of the Loman home. Miller creates a trope for the decline of the natural world. Towering apartments, radiating *"an angry glow of orange"* (p. 11), surround the home, allowing only a minimal amount of blue light from the sky to fall upon their property. Later, Willy fondly reminisces about lilacs, wisteria, peonies, and daffodils. He tries to plant seeds, impossible though such an effort to reconnect himself with the organic rhythms of the universe proves to be. The plight of the Lomans, then, finds its parallels in the architecture and urban space of their home. In text and performances, Miller insists on maintaining the drama's essential contrariety: *"An air of the dream clings to the place, a dream rising out of reality"* (p. 11), though reality ensures that Willy never fulfills his dreams, and his dreams never fully square with reality. Miller juxtaposes an imploding urban landscape of time present—"Smell the stink from that apartment house!" (p. 18)—with Willy's longings for a pastoral landscape, one necessarily reconstructed only in time past.

In order to understand the identity crises of Miller's tragic characters in *Death of A Salesman*, and especially the late, climactic scene in which Biff confronts Willy with the truth, it is necessary to understand shame's relation to guilt and identity. It is the confrontation with feelings of shame that enables Biff to find himself, separate his sense of identity from that of his father, and empathize with his father. Moreover, it is the denial of such feelings that cripples Willy and the rest of the Loman family. (...)

Biff understands his relation to others, notably his father, only after he literally goes unnoticed and unidentified by someone he thought would recognize him: Bill Oliver. Biff comes to the realization that there is no reason why Oliver should have recognized him, given that he couldn't recognize himself. That is, as Biff says to Happy, "I even believed myself that I'd been a salesman for him! And then he gave me one look and—I realized what a ridiculous lie my whole life has been! We've been talking in a dream for fifteen years. I was a shipping clerk" (104). Unlike his father's true self, which is immersed in shame and guilt, Biff's self surfaces and stays afloat because he learns about his guilt from his shame.

Willy's insistence that Biff is "spiting" him by not going to see Oliver prompts Biff to voice what he sees as the meaning behind his theft and his inability to face his old boss again: "I'm no good, can't you see what I am?" (113). In this case, it is not simply Biff's wrongdoing that makes him identify himself as "no good"; he has now grasped the fact that behind his habit of breaking the law lie feelings of shame. This question, "can't you see what I am?" represents the beginnings of Biff's separation of his own identity from that of his father. By the end of Act Two, Biff is certain, as he says to his brother, that "[t]he man don't know who we are!" At this point he is determined to force his father to "hear the truth—what you are and what I am!" (131, 130). He knows who he thought he was and, thus, why he stole Oliver's pen. As he reveals to his whole family.

> I stopped in the middle of that building and I saw—the sky. I saw the things that I love in this world. The work and the food and time to sit and smoke. And I looked at the pen and said to myself, what the hell am I grabbing this for? Why am I trying to become what I don't want to be? What am I doing in an office, making a contemptuous, begging fool of myself, when all I want is out there, waiting for me the minute I say I know who I am! Why can't I say that, Willy? *He tries to make Willy face him, but Willy pulls away and moves to the left.* (132)

"Willy," the father who has been transformed from "Dad" into simply a man in his son's eyes, cannot bear to have his dreams, and his heroic vision of his son, himself, and his own brother and father—the vision by which he lives and dies—exposed. Therefore, he "*pulls away*" in shame, before standing his ground and yelling, "*with hatred, threateningly,*" "The door of your life is wide open!" (132). Unlike the scene in the restaurant, in which Biff presents Happy with "*the rolled-up hose*" with which Willy intends to commit suicide and tells his brother that he "can't bear to look at his [father's] face!" out of shame (115), this time Biff does not turn away from his father. He insists on the truth being truly heard by his father. It is only after he realizes that this is an impossibility that "*he pulls away*" (133): "There's no spite in it any more. I'm just what I am, that's all" (133), says the son to his father. He now knows that he is "nothing" only under the umbrella of his father's destructive vision.

By the end of Act Two, Biff has a relatively clear understanding of who he is or, at the very least, who he is not. "I am not a leader of men," he says to his father in a "*fury,*" before "*he breaks down, sobbing*" (132–33). But his father cannot empathize with him because he is incapable of facing his own feelings of guilt and shame. To Willy, Biff's tears symbolize simply his son's love, and not, in any way, the struggle to separate from him. Biff demonstrates that he does in fact love his father, but, at the same time, this love is balanced by the recognition that if there is any chance of saving himself and his father he must leave home for good. The complexity of his feelings for his father goes unrecognized, however. Willy's response to Biff's breakdown is, "Oh, Biff! *Staring wildly*: He cried! Cried to me. *He is choking with his love, and now cries out his promise*: That boy—that boy is going to be magnificent!" (133).

What Biff wants from his father he ends up giving, without getting it back. He wants not only love, but empathy. Moreover, after confronting his own shame and discovering who he is not—that is, not the "boy" his father believes him to be—Biff demonstrates his ability to separate from his father and, consequently, his ability to empathize with him. (...)

In "Requiem," the final moments of Miller's tragedy, Biff is alone in his empathic understanding. Even Charley does not understand the meaning of Biff's final words about his father. "He had the wrong dreams. All, all, wrong. [...] He never knew who he was" (138, intervening dialogue omitted). Happy is *"ready to fight"* after these words, and Charley responds by saying to Biff, "Nobody dast blame this man. You don't understand: Willy was a salesman." But, as Linda suggests prior to this statement by Charley, "He was so wonderful with his hands," and it is this very suggestion that triggers Biff's final words about his father (138). Willy Loman was more himself, relatively free of guilt and shame, when he worked with his hands than at any other time in his life.

Driven by shame, he kills himself in order to preserve his dream of being "well liked" and a successful father and salesman. Of course, the irony is that because of his suicide the odds are very good that neither of his sons will benefit from his sacrifice, and nobody from his world of sales comes to his funeral. Linda's words at the end of the play, and especially the words, "We're free and clear" (139), reveal the degree to which she and her husband lived in denial, in fear of exposing the man who hid in shame behind the idea of being a successful salesman and father. To be "free and clear" is, ultimately, an impossibility for Willy Loman. His vision of success perpetuates crippling feelings of inferiority and inadequacy that drive him to destroy himself.

Unlike Biff, Willy does not confront and come to terms with his shame, and therefore he can never understand his guilt, nor his son's pain and his own responsibility for it. In "Tragedy and the Common Man," Miller states that "In [tragedies], and in them alone, lies the belief—optimistic, if you will, in the perfectibility of man."[7] In *Death of A Salesman*, he suggests, perhaps unintentionally, that the path to "perfection" lies in a confrontation with feelings of shame that enable one to understand guilt and arrive at a clearer sense of identity, as well as to empathize with others.

Notes

7. Arthur Miller, "Tragedy and the Common Man," in *The Theater Essays of Arthur Miller*, ed. Robert A. Martin (New York: Viking, 1978), 7.

Works by Arthur Miller

Situation Normal, 1944.

Focus, 1945.

All My Sons, 1947.

Death of a Salesman: Certain Private Conversations in Two Acts and a Requiem, 1949.

An Enemy of the People by Henrik Ibsen (adaptor), 1951.

The Crucible, 1953.

A View from the Bridge (with *A Memory of Two Mondays*): Two One-Act Plays, 1955.

Collected Plays, 1957–81. 2 vols.

The Misfits, 1961.

Jane's Blanket, 1963.

After the Fall, 1964.

Incident at Vichy, 1965.

I Don't Need You Anymore: Stories, 1967, 1987 (as *The Misfits and Other Stories*).

The Price, 1968.

In Russia (with Inge Morath), 1969.

The Portable Arthur Miller. Ed. Harold Clurman, 1971.

The Creation of the World and Other Business, 1973.

In the Country (with Inge Morath), 1977.

Theatre Essays. Ed. Robert A. Martin, 1978.

Chinese Encounters (with Inge Morath), 1979.

Eight Plays, 1981.

Playing for Time: A Screenplay, 1981.

The American Clock, 1982.

Elegy for a Lady, 1982.

Some Kind of Love Story, 1983.

The Archbishop's Ceiling, 1984.

Two-Way Mirror: A Double-Bill Elegy for a Lady and Some Kind of Love Story, 1984.

Playing for Time: A Full-Length Stage Play, 1985.

"Salesman" in Beijing, 1984.

Danger: Memory! A Double-Bill of I Can't Remember Anything and Clara, 1986.

Timebends: A Life, 1987.

Conversations with Arthur Miller. Ed. Matthew C. Roudané, 1987.

Plays: One, 1988.

The Archbishop's Ceiling; The American Clock, 1988.

Plays: Two, 1988.

The Golden Years and The Man Who Had All the Luck, 1989.

Early Plays, 1989.

On Censorship and Laughter, 1990.

Plays: Three, 1990.

Everybody Wins: A Screenplay, 1990.

The Last Yankee, 1991.

The Ride Down Mount Morgan, 1991.

Homely Girl: A Life (with Louis Bourgeois), 1992. 2 vols.

Broken Glass, 1994.

The Last Yankee; with a New Essay, About Theatre Language; and Broken Glass, 1994.

Plays: Four, 1994.

Arthur Miller: an Interview. BBC, 1997.

Mr. Peter's Connections, 1999.

Echoes Down the Corridor: Collected Essays, 1947–2000. Ed. Steven R. Centola, 2000.

On Politics And The Art of Acting, 2001.

Annotated Bibliography

Bigsby, Christopher, ed. *The Cambridge Companion to Arthur Miller*. Cambridge: Cambridge University Press, 1997.

The Cambridge Companion series is an excellent source for diverse essays on major writers. This study of Miller includes criticism of Miller's recent work as well as his major and familiar plays. The perspective of these essays encompasses the impact on the writer of the major social and political events that occur during his or her lifetime. The editor, Christopher Bigsby, is a prominent scholar of drama in general and Miller in particular. The essay on *Death of a Salesman* by Matthew Roudané is a particularly useful piece of criticism covering themes, setting, characterizations, and language.

Carson, Neil. *Modern Dramatists: Arthur Miller*. New York: St. Martin's Press, 1982.

Following two chapters of biographical material, Carson devotes a chapter to each of Miller's plays and one to his non-theatrical writing. Writing about *Death of a Salesman*, Carson emphasizes the three generations of the Loman family showing parallels and divergences. He offers an interesting look at the impact on audiences of the play's stage design and treatment of time. The book includes several photographs from play performances.

Corrigan, Robert W., ed. *Arthur Miller: A Collection of Critical Essays*. Englewood Cliffs, NJ: Prentice-Hall, Inc., 1969.

This book on Arthur Miller is part of the Twentieth Century Views series that consistently presents essays by outstanding teachers and critics. Published in 1969, its contributors reflect on the two decades of developing patterns and ideas in Miller's work since the 1949 performance of *Death of a Salesman*.

Freedman, Morris. *American Drama* in *Social Context*. Carbondale and Edwardsville: Southern Illinois University Press, 1971.

This study of American drama has a chapter on Arthur Miller's plays with an emphasis on their "Jewishness." When discussing *Death of a Salesman*, Freedman looks closely at the issues of family guilt and the relationship between Willy and his two sons.

Hayman, Ronald. *Contemporary Playwrights: Arthur Miller*. London: Heinemann Educational Books, Ltd., 1970.

Hayman begins with an interview he conducted with Miller—part of which appeared in *The Times* of February 15, 1969. He asks Miller to comment on his reaction to different performances of his plays and about his intentions for each. Writing about *Death of a Salesman*, which he calls the "best American play ever written," Hayman follows scene by scene commenting on the contribution of each character to the play's effect on the American theatre.

Hogan, Robert. *Arthur Miller*. Minneapolis: University of Minnesota Press, 1964.

This booklet is one of a series of pamphlets on American writers put out by the University of Minnesota Press. It reviews Miller's life and his important work up to 1964. Hogan begins by naming the two traditions of tragedy in Western literature—the austere and the experimental—and argues that Miller's work has elements of both. Hogan includes some interesting details about Miller's radio plays, his famous interaction with the House on Un-American Activities Committee and Joe McCarthy, and his marriage (ending in divorce) to Marilyn Monroe.

Miller, Arthur. *"Salesman" in Beijing*. New York: Viking Press, 1984.

This is the log Miller kept each day while rehearsing *Death of a Salesman* in Beijing. People interested in China, American/Chinese relations, cultural differences, Arthur

Miller, and/or the effects of the Cultural Revolution on Chinese artists and intellectuals would probably find his account highly useful. Miller was accompanied by his wife Inge Morath who spoke Chinese and took the numerous photographs of the play-in-progress.

Moss, Leonard. *Arthur Miller*. Boston: G. K. Hall & Co., 1980.

Leonard Moss has been reading and writing about Miller since his graduate school years. In this volume he diverges from the critical view of Miller as a social reformer and attempts to show that Miller's ideas about justice and the right values for living are never explicit but rather embedded in the psychological complexity of his characters and their social interactions. In 11979 Moss visited Miller at his Connecticut home to conduct an interview, which is included in the Appendix.

Murphy, Brenda. *Miller: "Death of a Salesman."* Cambridge: Cambridge University Press, 1995.

Murphy's book focuses entirely on the productions of *Death of a Salesman* beginning in 1949. She discusses Miller's early thinking about the play, the play's origins, and gives details of his working with first director Elia Kazan and set designer Jo Mielziner, actor tryouts, and critical responses. Illustrations from all the important productions—those in English as well as in foreign languages—are included. Especially interesting is the story of the film version of the play including the measures Columbia Pictures took to eliminate any hint of political message or suggestion that Willy Loman was typical of the American labor force. A discography, videography, and 31-page bibliography on Miller are also included.

Nelson, Benjamin. *Arthur Miller: Portrait of a Playwright*. London: Owen, 1970.

Nelson combines biography and literary criticism in his study of Miller. Details from Miller's early life, his work in a warehouse, and his literary interests and accomplishments in college are presented as the original material that later emerges in the plays. Nelson has two chapters on *Death of a Salesman*—one focused on its origins and production details, the other on its themes and the meaning Willy Loman has for American culture. Nelson's book is comprehensive and enjoyable to read. He appreciates Miller and his scene-by-scene analysis is full of insight.

Porter, Thomas E. *Myth and Modern American Drama*. Detroit: Wayne State University Press, 1969.

Porter's study addresses American drama using the foundations of Greek drama to establish a more precise way for defining terms and meanings. Two essays focus on Miller. The chapter on *Death of a Salesman* discusses the evolution of the American Dream concept with a view to its impact on each character in the play.

Roudané, Matthew C., ed. *Approaches to Teaching Miller's "Death of a Salesman."* New York: The Modern Language Association of America, 1995.

This collection of essays is excellent and unusual. The contributors—all teachers at the college level—are experienced at presenting Miller to diverse student populations. In the introductory section of the book, Roudané presents a list of bibliographies and a review of the collections of essays and other commentary on Miller that may be useful to teachers. Analyses of various performances and specific themes are taken up from feminist and class perspectives. Some examples include Paula Cohen who approaches the play as an example of paradigm shift in American history; James Hurt who writes about the Lomans in a family dynamics context; and June Schlueter who takes a postmodern view and questions whether Willy Loman's reveries are actual memories or "constructs." She also supplies a carefully prepared chronology of the play which encourages multiple interpretations of Willy's story.

Welland, Dennis. *Arthur Miller*. New York: Grove Press, Inc., 1961.

Welland's first chapter is biographical and includes detailed information surrounding the refusal of the U.S. Department of State in 1954 to issue a passport to Miller for travel to Brussels for the opening there of *The Crucible*. His chapter on *Death of a Salesman* is especially interesting for its review and discussion of the divergent opinions generated by the play about the American Dream and the capitalist system.

Contributors

Harold Bloom is Sterling Professor of the Humanities at Yale University and Henry W. and Albert A. Berg Professor of English at the New York University Graduate School. He is the author of over 20 books, including *Shelley's Mythmaking* (1959), *The Visionary Company* (1961), *Blake's Apocalypse* (1963), *Yeats* (1970), *A Map of Misreading* (1975), *Kabbalah and Criticism* (1975), *Agon: Toward a Theory of Revisionism* (1982), *The American Religion* (1992), *The Western Canon* (1994), and *Omens of Millennium: The Gnosis of Angels, Dreams, and Resurrection* (1996). *The Anxiety of Influence* (1973) sets forth Professor Bloom's provocative theory of the literary relationships between the great writers and their predecessors. His most recent books include *Shakespeare: The Invention of the Human* (1998), a 1998 National Book Award finalist, *How to Read and Why* (2000), *Genius: A Mosaic of One Hundred Exemplary Creative Minds* (2002), and *Hamlet: Poem Unlimited* (2003). In 1999, Professor Bloom received the prestigious American Academy of Arts and Letters Gold Medal for Criticism, and in 2002 he received the Catalonia International Prize.

Portia Williams Weiskel has taught English and journalism in both high school and adult education atmospheres, and has done freelance copyediting for numerous colleges. Her publications include writings on Joyce, Tolstoy, and Wilder.

Mary McCarthy was one of America's prominent intellectuals who spoke out on politics and hypocrisy. She is best known as author of *The Group* (1963) and her memoir *Memories of a Catholic Girlhood* (1957).

Tom Driver taught theology and literature at Union Theological Seminary in New York City. His published work includes *The Sense of History in Greek and Shakespearean Drama* (1960) and *Jean Genet* (1966).

Dennis Welland taught literature at Manchester University in England; he was a leading figure in establishing American Studies as a discipline in Great Britain.

Eric Mottram was a lecturer in American literature at the Institute of U.S. Studies at King's College, University of London. In 1966 he had a visiting lectureship at New York University. Mottram was a published poet and former editor of *Poetry Review*.

In addition to his work on Miller, **Benjamin Nelson** in 1962 edited and wrote the preface to a new translation of Soren Kierkegaard's writings.

Leonard Moss is Professor Emeritus at SUNY at Geneseo. In 2000 he published *The Excess of Heroism in Tragic Drama*.

Arguably the greatest American dramatist of the twentieth century, **Arthur Miller** is best known for also producing such classics as *The Crucible* and *A View from the Bridge*. He has written screenplays for Hollywood as well as collections of criticism.

Brenda Murphy is Professor of Literature at the University of Connecticut. She received a research grant for this book from the National Endowment for the Humanities.

Matthew Roudané is Professor of English at Georgia State University in Atlanta. He edited *Conversations with Arthur Miller* (1987), *Approaches to Teaching Miller's "Death of a Salesman"* (1995), and *The Cambridge Companion to Sam Shepard* (2002).

Fred Ribkoff teaches literature at the University of British Columbia.

Acknowledgments

"Preface" by Mary McCarthy. From *Sights and Spectacles*, 1956: xiv–xvi. © 1956 by Farrar, Straus and Cudahy. Reprinted by permission.

"Strength and Weakness in Arthur Miller" by Tom Driver. From *The Tulane Drama Review* 4, no. 4 (1960): 49–50. © 1960 by *The Tulane Drama Review*. Reprinted by permission.

"*Death of a Salesman*" by Dennis Welland. From *Arthur Miller*, 1961: 53–56. © 1961 by Dennis Welland. Reprinted by permission.

"Arthur Miller: the Development of a Political Dramatist in America" by Eric Mottram. From *A Collection of Critical Essays*, ed. Robert W. Corrigan, 1969: 23–24, 29–33. © 1969 by 1969 by Prentice Hall, Inc. Reprinted by permission.

" 'I am not a dime a dozen'" by Benjamin Nelson. From *Arthur Miller: Portrait of a Playwright*, 1970: 108–110. © 1970 by Benjamin Nelson. Reprinted by permission.

Arthur Miller by Leonard Moss: 25–26. © 1980 by G. K. Hall & Co. Reprinted by permission of the Gale Group.

"*Salesman*" in *Beijing* by Arthur Miller, 1984: 43–44, 49, 79–80, 86–87. © 1984 by Arthur Miller. Reprinted by permission.

"General Preface" by Brenda Murphy. From *Miller: "Death of a Salesman,"* 1995: 4–7. © 1995 by Cambridge University Press. Reprinted with the permission of Cambridge University Press.

"*Death of a Salesman* and the poetics of Arthur Miller" by Matthew Roudané. From *The Cambridge Companion to Arthur*

Index

.